This book was very loved
But we needed room for new.

TEEN RIGHTS AND FREEDOMS

Labor and Employment

TEEN RIGHTS AND FREEDOMS

Labor and Employment

David Haugen and Susan Musser
Book Editors

GREENHAVEN PRESS
A part of Gale, Cengage Learning

Detroit • New York • San Francisco • New Haven, Conn • Waterville, Maine • London

Elizabeth Des Chenes, *Director, Publishing Solutions*

© 2013 Greenhaven Press, a part of Gale, Cengage Learning

Gale and Greenhaven Press are registered trademarks used herein under license.

For more information, contact:
Greenhaven Press
27500 Drake Rd.
Farmington Hills, MI 48331-3535
Or you can visit our Internet site at gale.cengage.com.

For product information and technology assistance, contact us at:

Gale Customer Support, 1-800-877-4253.
For permission to use material from this text or product, submit all requests online at www.cengage.com/permissions.

Further permissions questions can be emailed to permissionrequest@cengage.com.

Articles in Greenhaven Press anthologies are often edited for length to meet page requirements. In addition, original titles of these works are changed to clearly present the main thesis and to explicitly indicate the author's opinion. Every effort is made to ensure the Greenhaven Press accurately reflects the original intent of the authors. Every effort has been made to trace the owners of copyrighted material.

Cover Image © mangostock/Shutterstock.com.

LIBRARY OF CONGRESS CATALOGING-IN-PUBLICATION DATA

Labor and employment / David Haugen and Susan Musser, book editors
    p. cm. -- (Teen rights and freedoms.)
    Includes bibliographical references and index.
    ISBN 978-0-7377-6402-4 (hardcover)
    1. Child labor--Law and legislation--United States. 2. Teenagers--Legal status, laws, etc.--United States. 3. Teenagers--Employment--United States. I. Haugen, David M., 1969- II. Musser, Susan.
    KF3552.L33 2012
344.7301'31--dc23

                                                                        2012008968

Printed in the United States of America
1 2 3 4 5 6 7 16 15 14 13 12

Contents

Foreword

"In the truest sense freedom cannot be bestowed, it must be achieved."
Franklin D. Roosevelt,
September 16, 1936

The notion of children and teens having rights is a relatively recent development. Early in American history, the head of the household—nearly always the father—exercised complete control over the children in the family. Children were legally considered to be the property of their parents. Over time, this view changed, as society began to acknowledge that children have rights independent of their parents, and that the law should protect young people from exploitation. By the early twentieth century, more and more social reformers focused on the welfare of children, and over the ensuing decades advocates worked to protect them from harm in the workplace, to secure public education for all, and to guarantee fair treatment for youths in the criminal justice system. Throughout the twentieth century, rights for children and teens—and restrictions on those rights—were established by Congress and reinforced by the courts. Today's courts are still defining and clarifying the rights and freedoms of young people, sometimes expanding those rights and sometimes limiting them. Some teen rights are outside the scope of public law and remain in the realm of the family, while still others are determined by school policies.

Each volume in the Teen Rights and Freedoms series focuses on a different right or freedom and offers an anthology of key essays and articles on that right or freedom and the responsibilities that come with it. Material within each volume is drawn from a diverse selection of primary and secondary sources—journals, magazines, newspapers, nonfiction books, organization newsletters, position papers, speeches, and government documents, with a particular emphasis on Supreme Court and lower court decisions. Volumes also include first-person narratives from young people and others involved in teen rights issues, such as parents and educators. The material is selected and arranged to highlight all the major social and legal controversies relating to the right or freedom under discussion. Each selection is preceded by an introduction that provides context and background. In many cases, the essays point to the difference between adult and teen rights, and why this difference exists.

Many of the volumes cover rights guaranteed under the Bill of Rights and how these rights are interpreted and protected in regard to children and teens, including freedom of speech, freedom of the press, due process, and religious rights. The scope of the series also encompasses rights or freedoms, whether real or perceived, relating to the school environment, such as electronic devices, dress, Internet policies, and privacy. Some volumes focus on the home environment, including topics such as parental control and sexuality.

Numerous features are included in each volume of Teen Rights and Freedoms:

- An annotated **table of contents** provides a brief summary of each essay in the volume and highlights court decisions and personal narratives.
- An **introduction** specific to the volume topic gives context for the right or freedom and its impact on daily life.
- A brief **chronology** offers important dates associated with the right or freedom, including landmark court cases.
- **Primary sources**—including personal narratives and court decisions—are among the varied selections in the anthology.
- **Illustrations**—including photographs, charts, graphs, tables, statistics, and maps—are closely tied to the text and chosen to help readers understand key points or concepts.

- An annotated list of **organizations to contact** presents sources of additional information on the topic.
- A **for further reading** section offers a bibliography of books, periodical articles, and Internet sources for further research.
- A comprehensive subject **index** provides access to key people, places, events, and subjects cited in the text.

Each volume of Teen Rights and Freedoms delves deeply into the issues most relevant to the lives of teens: their own rights, freedoms, and responsibilities. With the help of this series, students and other readers can explore from many angles the evolution and current expression of rights both historic and contemporary.

Introduction

In a mid-November 2011 address at Harvard University's Kennedy School of Government, Republican presidential candidate Newt Gingrich stirred controversy by telling an audience that US child labor laws are "truly stupid," leaving most youth in disadvantaged neighborhoods devoid of the work habits that might help them escape poverty. Based on his belief that US schools are failing children in poor communities, Gingrich stated, "Most of these schools ought to get rid of the unionized janitors, have one master janitor and pay local students to take care of the school. The kids would actually do work, they would have cash, they would have pride in the schools, they'd begin the process of rising." On December 1, at a meeting in Iowa, he expounded on his views by insisting that poor children grow up in environments in which they do not understand the fundamentals of traditional work: "They have no habit of staying [at a job] all day. They have no habit of 'I do this and you give me cash,' unless it's illegal." According to the *Los Angeles Times*, Gingrich said "he favored putting children to work in paid jobs at the schools they attend 'as early as is reasonable and practical.'" He had previously mentioned that children as young as nine might take over janitorial duties in schools.

The remarks drew fire from liberal political commentators as well as child advocates. In a December 14, 2011, article in the *Charlotte Observer*, reporter Fannie Flono argues, "The Republican presidential candidate's claim that child labor laws are 'truly stupid' rightly offends many people." After dismissing what she sees as Gingrich's erroneous claim that disadvantaged youth have no working role models, Flono writes,

> It should still appall us that he thinks poor children as young as 10 should work 20 hours a week as janitors. The idea is nothing to cheer. At the turn of the 20th century, it became

appallingly evident that children were being exploited as laborers in this country—often working under dangerous circumstances. Gingrich's idea that kids work as school janitors doesn't improve upon that situation. School janitors don't just sweep floors. They operate machinery, work with electrical systems, and do all kinds of jobs that require skill, dexterity and judgment that young people don't have.

StudentsFirst, a grassroots movement to revamp the education system, quickly posted a petition that echoed Flono's sentiments and called upon Americans to register their disagreement with Gingrich's scheme. Both Flono and StudentsFirst contend that getting a good education, not manual labor, is the key to escaping poverty.

As Flono points out, opposition to child labor came to national attention in the United States in the early twentieth century. Citing the lack of education, the absence of a relatively carefree childhood, and the long working hours in often dangerous jobs in factories, reformers spent decades trying to convince lawmakers, judicial bodies, and the public that too many young people were being exploited for their cheap labor. In a 1923 debate over a proposed constitutional amendment to ban child labor, Senator Medill McCormick of Illinois made his reasons for endorsement plain:

> We have been gratified to believe here there was for every child a greater opportunity than elsewhere in the world; that here there was a higher average well-being, and a greater average intelligence than elsewhere in the world. Now we find ourselves checked and shocked by the knowledge that as a people we are powerless to assure to the children of America, the freedom from drudgery, from industrial slavery, necessary for their health, their growth, their schooling and their future citizenship.

Though Congress never approved an amendment, the legislature did adopt the Fair Labor Standards Act (FLSA) in 1938 that limited child labor in the United States.

Some critics have argued that the child labor rules in the FLSA came about partly through a changing conception of childhood that had been evolving and progressing since the nineteenth century. As Senator McCormick's words demonstrate, by the early 1900s, many saw children as underdeveloped individuals in need of guidance, education, and good health—and childhood was a distinct period from adulthood. In his 1962 book *Centuries of Childhood*, French historian Philippe Ariès maintains this had not always been the case. In previous centuries, children often went into work by age seven, and the entrance into labor signaled maturity into the responsibilities of adulthood. Only the children of the wealthy could afford to live in relative idleness; working-class families and farm families needed income, and their children typically joined trades or, by the Industrial Revolution, went to work in factories and mines. Ironically, it was during the Victorian Era—when factory work dominated Western economies—that reformers in England began pushing for child labor laws. Many of these reformers, especially Christian groups, were appalled by the hazardous or squalid working conditions in factories, and these advocates stressed that children should be protected from harm because of their innocence and helplessness. In addition, the reform movement was aided by a growing middle class because the children of shopkeepers could afford to have more leisure and time to pursue education. This transition supports Ariès's claim that childhood is a modern invention that did not spread until the nineteenth and twentieth centuries.

Today, the concept of child labor invokes conflicting images, emotions, and philosophies. For many, the term conjures up photographs of children toiling in industry—imagery that steels one against the idea of exploiting the innocent. For others, like Newt Gingrich, children should have the opportunity, if not the explicit right, to better themselves through work. From one stance, economic activity is a way toward maturity and improvement; to others, a focus on money is a distraction from childhood and may irreparably taint young people in years to come.

The authors in *Teen Rights and Freedoms: Labor and Employment* examine the issues surrounding child labor and illustrate the ongoing debate over the advantages and harms of allowing children to work.

Chronology

1832
The New England Association of Farmers, Mechanics and Other Workingmen publically criticizes child labor practices that force children to work in factories all day long without any breaks as harmful to the youths' health and well-being.

1836
Massachusetts passes the first child labor law, which mandates a minimum of three months of schooling per year for all children up to fifteen years of age who work in factories.

1842
Individual states begin passing laws setting limits with regards to how many hours per day a child can work; however, the enforcement of these laws varies.

April 25, 1904
The National Child Labor Committee forms with the goal of exposing the harsh working conditions faced by children in industrial factories and advocating for an end to the practice.

September 1, 1916
The US Congress approves the Keating-Owen Child Labor Act of 1916. The legislation makes it illegal to sell or purchase goods made by child laborers across interstate lines.

June 3, 1918	In the US Supreme Court case *Hammer v. Dagenhart*, the court rules the Keating-Owen Child Labor Act of 1916 is unconstitutional and states that the federal government cannot interfere with how states choose to regulate child labor or the goods it produces.
1919	With the passage of the 1919 Child Labor Tax Law, any individual or business employing workers under the age of fourteen, or having children age fourteen to sixteen work more than eight hours a day or six days a week, must pay a 10 percent excise tax.
May 15, 1922	The US Supreme Court rules that the 1919 Child Labor Tax Law is unconstitutional, finding the tax to be a penalty for employing minors.
1936	Part of the New Deal, the Walsh Healey Public Contracts Act prohibits the government from purchasing goods fabricated by underage children (women under eighteen and men under sixteen).
1938	US Congress passes the Fair Labor Standards Act of 1938, which, along with setting wage guarantees for all employees, becomes the first federal legislation to establish guidelines regarding the conditions under which children

may be employed and the wages they
must receive.

February 3, 1941
In *United States v. Darby Lumber Co.,*
the US Supreme Court overturns
Hammer v. Dagenhart, maintain-
ing that the Fair Labor Standards
Act of 1938 is constitutional and the
US Congress can pass legislation
mandating certain conditions in the
workplace.

January 31, 1944
In *Prince v. Massachusetts,* the US
Supreme Court rules that parents are
prohibited from forcing their children
to work under conditions that violate
existing laws governing child labor.

November 20, 1989
The United Nations passes the
Convention on the Rights of the Child,
which states that minors should not be
allowed to perform work that may be
detrimental to their physical and men-
tal well-being.

1992
Democratic US senator from Iowa,
Tom Harkin, introduces the Child
Labor Deterrence Act, which would ban
US companies from importing goods
manufactured with child labor; the bill
fails to pass.

June 17, 1999
The International Labour Organization
adopts the Worst Forms of Child
Labour Convention, which calls on

participating countries to actively outlaw and seek to eradicate the worst forms of child labor including slavery, sexual exploitation, and use of children for illicit activities such as drug trafficking.

> "Sometime between the two world
> wars . . . moral legitimacy had passed
> from those in favor of unrestricted
> child labor to those favoring highly
> regulated, supervised forms of juvenile
> money-making."

Regulating Child Labor in the United States: An Overview

Todd Postol

The issue of child labor in the United States gained national attention in the Progressive Era of the early twentieth century. In the following viewpoint, Todd Postol explains how various crusaders brought to public attention the dangerous conditions in which young workers often toiled in US industries. Gaining larger support, these early reform movements sparked state legislation to limit working hours and hazardous employment for children, Postol writes. However, even though national attitudes were changing by the 1920s and 1930s, Postol maintains that federal laws were slow to take shape, and the US Supreme Court struck down attempts to endow the US Congress with the power to regulate child labor. Postol states that the passage of the Fair Labor Standards Act in 1938 finally defined federal statutes on child labor, but since then the issue has faded from the national spotlight, leaving enforcement of the law lax and violations more commonplace. Postol is a history professor.

Todd Postol, "Public Health and Working Children in Twentieth-Century America: An Historical Review," *Journal of Public Health Policy*, Autumn 1993, pp. 348–354. Copyright © 1993 by Palgrave Macmillan. All rights reserved. Reproduced by permission.

Throughout this century, concern for the health of America's youth has been a driving force in the long fight to regulate child labor in the United States. In 1900, according to the federal census, more than 1.7 million children were gainfully employed, an increase of more than a million over the preceding three decades. Since the census excluded children under 10, and did not accurately record thousands of youngsters hawking newspapers and shining shoes, the true number of working children in America was far higher than the reported total. In New York state alone, one scholar has estimated, 400,000 children between the ages of 5 and 18 were in the labor force.

Early Crusaders for Children's Safety at Work

Children at the turn of the century could be found working without benefit of the most basic health and safety protection in nearly every major industry. Although 28 states had some child labor law on their books, statutes typically regulated only the ages and hours children could work; as long as these standards were not violated, employers could and did work minors as they saw fit. In lower Manhattan, girls suffered permanent spinal damage as they sat for long, uninterrupted stretches hunched over their sewing tables. In Indiana, boys toiled in glass factories without masks or adequate ventilation. And in the mills of the southeast, youngsters worked 12-hour days in deafening, lint-filled spinning rooms.

State investigators had known of these deplorable conditions since the mid-19th century, but the American public was largely unaware of the necessity for stricter legal safeguards. One of the first people to focus attention on the problem was labor organizer Mary "Mother" Jones. On May 29, 1903, 100,000 textile workers, including 16 thousand children below 16, walked off their jobs at mills in and around Philadelphia. Strikers were demanding a reduction in the work week from 60 to 55 hours. The following month Jones arrived in the city's Kensington district and found, as she later recalled, little children, "some with their hands off, some with their fingers off at the knuckle. They were stooped little things, round shouldered and skinny." Despite the fact that Pennsylvania prohibited children under 13 from working, many of the children Jones saw were below 10. Jones assembled a group of maimed children before city hall: "I called upon the millionaire manufacturers to cease their moral murders," she noted in her autobiography, but Philadelphia officials literally closed their windows, "just as they had closed their eyes and hearts." Jones' reaction was swift: she organized a fife and drum "children's crusade" of nearly 300 marchers, and set off on July 7, 1903 to present her case to the President of the United States at his summer mansion 125 miles away on Long Island. Along the way, Jones lectured students at Princeton: "Here's a text book on economics," she said, pointing to a stooped ten-year-old boy, "he gets three dollars a week and his sister who is fourteen gets six dollars. They work in a carpet factory ten hours a day while the children of the rich are getting their higher education." By the time the crusade reached the locked gates of [US president] Theodore Roosevelt's estate at Oyster Bay, heat and distance had depleted its ranks to just a half-dozen stalwarts, but Jones had accomplished her goal of drawing national attention to the health risks faced by working children.

State Legislation on Child Labor Varies

The year before the march, a group of prominent New York educators, reformers and physicians came together to found the New York Child Labor Committee. In just one year, the Committee persuaded Albany to pass five landmark pieces of legislation preventing the employment of very young children. Under the bills, children were required to furnish proof of their age before being hired for factory work. This made it more difficult for young children to lie about their ages in order to get a job. A 9-hour day was mandated for 14- and 15-year-olds, and any child under 16 wishing to work in an office, factory, or store had to first obtain a state work certificate.

While these bills restricted access to factory and retail work, they did not eliminate across-the-board child labor. Opposition to a street trades bill weakened the state's badge system to the point where it was unenforceable. Huge numbers of children in tenement homework and agriculture were also beyond the reach of regulation.

For all their deficiencies, the New York child labor bills of 1903 were an impressive Progressive-era legislative success. But they applied only to one state, and few other states were able to match New York's achievements. Some, like Massachusetts and Wisconsin, were extending the scope of protection for child laborers; the country as a whole, however, was a patchwork of loosely written, poorly enforced laws. In response to the need for collective action, reformers banded together to form the National Child Labor Committee in 1904. Over the next forty years it would be in the forefront of the struggle to eliminate child labor in the United States.

Armed with statistics, maps, and testimony, Progressive reformers fought an industry-by-industry war to publicize the detrimental effects of child labor. Progress was slow. In 1909 the persistent efforts of the New York Committee resulted in the passage of the Voss Dangerous Trades Act. It prohibited children under 16 in more than 30 dangerous occupations. Reading the list today it hardly seems believable that anyone would have employed children in the manufacture of dynamite and matches, or used minors to adjust belts on moving machinery or run circular saws. A weakness of the Act was that employers could continue using children in those occupations not specifically designated by the Act as being dangerous. Thus, operating a heeling machine in a shoe factory was legal because the framers of the Voss Act had not termed it dangerous. Two years after the act was passed, 146 employees working behind locked doors, mostly women and girls, died in New York's infamous Triangle Shirtwaist fire.

Children work in a Georgia cotton mill in the early twentieth century. Photographs such as this, taken by social reformer Lewis Hine, brought national attention to the plight of child laborers. © Bettmann/Corbis/AP Images.

Incredibly, even after management had been brought to trial and the factory reopened, the company continued to lock girls in at work. No wonder early child labor reformers sometimes despaired of the glacial pace of improvement.

Photographs of Child Workers Spur National Concern

Though neither committee attempted anything as flamboyant as the children's crusade, the National Committee did hire a professional photographer. Lewis Hine began working in a Wisconsin furniture factory when he was orphaned at 15. After receiving a master's degree in education from the University of Chicago, Hine turned to photography as a way of chronicling the plight of the nation's poor. In his work for the National Committee, Hine used any excuse to get inside factories, mines and homes to photograph and interview children at work. His haunting prints were widely circulated by the Committee and later exhibited at museums and reproduced in national publications, including *Life* magazine.

Through its ties with Capitol Hill, the National Committee helped secure the establishment of the U.S. Children's Bureau in 1912. As part of the Department of Commerce and Labor, the Bureau had no administrative power, but it did have a modest budget for producing informational materials. It soon led the way in promoting maternal health, infant disease prevention, and school health programs. These issues interacted with the problem of child labor, but there was no national agency aimed at working children until 1916 when the Keating-Owen Act was signed into law by President [Woodrow] Wilson. The act prohibited the interstate commerce of goods produced by children under 14 and set an 8-hour day for working youngsters under 16. Responsibility for enforcement of the act was given to the Children's Bureau, which established a special Child Labor division. Nine months after it was put into place, the [US] Supreme Court ruled that Keating-Owen exceeded the federal government's power to regulate interstate trade, and the act was found unconstitutional. This setback signalled the end of classic Progressive-era child labor reform, and ushered in two decades of defeat and reversal at the national level.

Roadblock in the Reform Era

In 1919 a second federal child labor law was enacted, but it too was struck down by the Supreme Court. Returning to the states, reformers were increasingly successful in regulating child labor in the larger industrial states. In the non-unionized south and in states where agriculture played a big role in the economy, they were less successful. Throughout the 1920s the National Committee tried, unsuccessfully, to pass a constitutional amendment outlawing child labor. With the coming of the New Deal, advocates of federal child labor reform finally met with partial success. In 1933 the National Recovery Administration [NRA] banned workers below 16 in most industries. The NRA addressed the question of occupational health head-on, by denying entrance in the so-called hazardous trades to employees under 18. In an all-too-familiar scenario, however, FDR's [US president Franklin Delano Roosevelt's] agency for economic recovery was invalidated by the Supreme Court in 1935.

Ironically, opponents of child labor were now on the verge of their greatest victory. Three years after the NRA was overturned, the Fair Labor Standards Act [FLSA] incorporated many of the same limitations on interstate commerce as the old Keating-Owen act. It raised the full-time working age to 16 and strictly limited the conditions of labor for 14- and 15-year olds. Like the NRA, the FLSA targeted "oppressive" child labor, using the health of the child as a primary criterion in outlawing dangerous work for minors. Unlike previous efforts, the FLSA was not invalidated. By 1940 the success of state legislation, automation, and the power of the federal government as exercised through the FLSA had severely limited the extent of child labor in the US. For the next three decades, in fact, historians would assume that child labor was a thing of the past and treat it as if it no longer existed. A more accurate way to think of the post-war years is to view them as the quiet decades, when child labor receded but did not disappear. Large numbers of children in migrant agriculture remained without legal protection well into the 1950s.

National Attitudes Shift Toward Protecting Children from Harm in the Mid-1930s

Before consideration of contemporary child labor, it might be helpful to pose the question: What part did publicizing dangerous abuses have in curbing child labor prior to the passage of the FLSA? Clearly it played a major, perhaps decisive role. Sometime between the two world wars, certainly by the close of the NRA, moral legitimacy had passed from those in favor of unrestricted child labor to those favoring highly regulated, supervised forms of juvenile money-making. Nowhere can this new relationship between childhood and work be seen more easily than in newspaper distribution—the one industry where children remained economically potent. Even though reformers and circulation managers continued to disagree on the proper role of minors in distributing the news, by the mid-1930s *both* groups were couching their arguments in the language of promoting healthy, responsible child development. An important element in this equation was the altered attitude of parents: fathers and mothers now rejected the very notion of work if there was any possibility that it might physically or emotionally harm their children.

Problems Reemerge Late in the Century

In recent decades this concern has eroded. Two trends have emerged which again make the topic of underage employment a subject of public discussion. First, the rise of the student-worker, virtually unknown outside North America, has led to a flood of complaints in the service sector that adolescents are illegally employed in dangerous occupations. Recently [in 1992], the *Washington Post* announced that the nation's fastest-growing supermarket chain, Food Lion, is about to be charged by the Labor Department with 1,400 violations of federal child labor law. More than 1,200 of the alleged violations involve minors "working around hazardous equipment such as meat slicers and package bailers". In addition to such obvious physical health risks, student-workers are also exposed to a host of social dangers: in their 1986 study, *When Teenagers Work*, Ellen Greenberger and Laurence Steinberg found that students who worked intensively throughout the school year were more likely to engage in deviant behavior, including "buying and using drugs and alcohol, cutting school, skipping classes [and] lying about the completion of assigned homework".

A second trend contributing to the revival of debate on child labor has been the re-emergence of illegal immigrant sweatshops in large metropolitan centers like New York and Los Angeles. During the 1980s, federal and state budgets for enforcing compliance with child labor laws were reduced. At the same time, there was a surge in immigration, particularly from Asia and Latin America, where child labor is an enduring problem. Specialists in the field of child labor believe that greater resources and commitment are needed to ensure the health of our children. With attention again focusing on the health of working minors, perhaps the 1990s will witness a renewal of the agenda for improving the lives of American children that was initiated with such enthusiasm at the beginning of this century.

| "The United States, through the FLSA and state laws, has adopted various restrictions to prevent the exploitation of child labor."

State and Federal Governments Address Child Labor in Different Ways

Andrea Giampetro-Meyer, Timothy Brown, and Nancy Kubasek

The Fair Labor Standards Act of 1938 placed federal limits on the age of working children and the type of jobs they could acquire. In the following viewpoint, Andrea Giampetro-Meyer, Timothy Brown, and Nancy Kubasek describe how state laws are similar and different from the federal statute. The authors claim that state laws are modeled on the FLSA, but instead of keeping children away from hazardous occupations, they tend to stress limiting work hours to ensure that work does not intrude on schooling. Giampetro-Meyer and Brown are law professors at Loyola College in Baltimore, Maryland. Kubasek is a law professor at Bowling Green State University in Ohio.

Regulation of child labor in the United States began in the early 1900s. By 1914, child labor committees existed in thirty-five states, and local committees were established in every major industrial center. Also, some type of child labor law had been enacted in forty states. In 1938, the Fair Labor Standards Act ("FLSA"), the federal law governing child labor, was enacted. The FLSA was designed to eliminate oppressive child labor by placing limits on the ages of employment, the hours children work, and the type of work they perform. In addition to this federal legislation, all fifty states and the District of Columbia have adopted child labor laws. . . .

The Scope of the Fair Labor Standards Act for Child Workers

While the FLSA has been amended six times since its enactment in 1938, the law regarding the age of employment has not changed. From 1938 through the present, the FLSA has defined oppressive child labor as employment of a child under sixteen years of age, except employment of children between fourteen and sixteen years of age in nonmining, nonhazardous, nonmanufacturing occupations and under conditions that the Secretary of Labor determines do not interfere with their schooling or well-being. For minors between the ages of sixteen and eighteen, the FLSA only prohibits work in nonagricultural occupations that are considered particularly hazardous or detrimental to their health or well-being.

The FLSA does not absolutely prohibit the employment of children under sixteen. These children may work for a parent, or a person standing in place of a parent, during non-school hours in occupations declared nonhazardous for minors under the age of eighteen. Moreover, children who are between the ages of fourteen and sixteen may be employed in agricultural occupations, as long as the work has not been declared hazardous for minors under eighteen and will be performed during non-school hours. Two other areas of work permitted for children

"Before I mow the grass, I'd like to quote from section four paragraph c, of the state child labor code," cartoon by Carroll Zahn. Reproduction rights obtainable from www .CartoonStock.com.

of any age are acting and delivering newspapers to consumers. Finally, an employer can apply to the Secretary of Labor for a waiver to employ children between ten and twelve years old as hand harvest laborers during the summer.

State Laws Vary but Usually Limit Work Hours for Children

State regulations of employment hours vary widely, with most laws focused on keeping students from dropping out of school. When establishing the maximum daily and weekly hours and the

Although state labor laws vary, most focus on limiting work hours for children to prevent students from dropping out of school. © Photodisc/Getty Images.

maximum days per week for minors under sixteen years of age, several state legislatures have followed the FLSA and have distinguished periods when school is in session from those when students are not in school.

In the majority of states, legislators typically limit the maximum number of hours a minor is allowed to work based on whether the work occurs during school periods. During non-school periods, legislators restrict children under the age of sixteen to an eight-hour workday. Some of these states that distinguish between school and non-school periods also limit the maximum number of hours per day that sixteen- and seventeen-year-olds may work when school is not in session. The maximum daily hours allowed when school is out of session is typically nine or ten. When school is in session, most states place the maximum daily work hours for minors under the age of sixteen at three or four. Some state restrictions are based on the combined hours of work and school, and allow eight to ten hours as the maximum number of hours. In states that do not distinguish between school and non-school periods, almost all limit the maximum daily hours for minors under age sixteen to eight hours. Some states limit the hours for sixteen- and seventeen-year-olds to nine or ten hours per day.

In sum, many states limit daily work hours for minors under age sixteen to eight hours. Some states place further restrictions by limiting these hours to a maximum of three per day when school is in session. States tend to be more lenient with sixteen- and seventeen-year-olds, either placing no limits on them or allowing them to work more hours than minors under sixteen years of age.

Most states also regulate the maximum weekly hours for minors under age sixteen. In states that distinguish between school and non-school periods, it is typical for the legislature to determine that minors under the age of sixteen may work forty hours per week when school is not in session, and eighteen hours per week during school periods. Some states allow minors who are not in school to work forty-eight hours per week.

For states that do not distinguish school and non-school periods, the typical maximum work hours per week for minors under age sixteen are either forty or forty-eight. Some states allow sixteen- or seventeen-year-olds to work up to fifty-four hours per week, even when school is in session.

All states place some limits on night work for minors under age sixteen, although their provisions vary considerably. Some states prohibit night work only during the school year, while the more protective states prohibit all work from nine o'clock in the evening to seven o'clock in the morning, even when school is not in session. Several states place no restrictions on the night work of sixteen- and seventeen-year-olds, while others enact regulations that reflect a concern that students should not perform night work.

Recently, some states have demonstrated increasing concern for the academic performance of working minors. For example, the New Hampshire legislature amended its Youth Employment law to require a satisfactory level of academic achievement before the state can issue a work certificate. If the working minor does not maintain a satisfactory level of academic achievement, the state must revoke the certificate. The New Hampshire legislature also placed restrictions on the number of hours that sixteen- and seventeen-year-olds may work during the school week. The state also created a committee to study the relationship between academic achievement and work.

Thus, the United States, through the FLSA and state laws, has adopted various restrictions to prevent the exploitation of child labor.

> "The grant of power to Congress over the subject of interstate commerce was to enable it to regulate such commerce, and not to give it authority to control the States."

Congress Does Not Have the Power to Regulate Child Labor Within States

The Supreme Court's Decision

William R. Day

In 1916, Congress passed the Keating-Owen Act of 1916, a law that prohibited the interstate commerce of goods manufactured in industries using child labor. Claiming the law was unconstitutional, Roland Dagenhart, representing his two young sons who worked in cotton mills in North Carolina, brought suit against the government. A US District Court ruled in Dagenhart's favor, leading US Attorney W.C. Hammer to appeal the case to the US Supreme Court. The following viewpoint is the majority opinion of the court as given by Associate Justice William R. Day. In it, Day upholds the lower court's ruling and deems the Keating-Owen Act unconstitutional. Day asserts that the Commerce Clause in Article 1 of the US Constitution regulates interstate transport and trade of goods

William R. Day, Majority opinion, *Hammer v. Dagenhart*, Supreme.Justia.com, June 3, 1918.

or services but does not regulate how products are manufactured. The court maintains that regulating the manufacture of goods is the sole discretion of the states. Therefore, the court concludes that the federal government has no authority to enact or enforce laws concerning child labor by appealing to the Commerce Clause.

A bill was filed in the United States District Court for the Western District of North Carolina by a father in his own behalf and as next friend of his two minor sons, one under the age of fourteen years and the other between the ages of fourteen and sixteen years, employees in a cotton mill at Charlotte, North Carolina, to enjoin the enforcement of the act of Congress intended to prevent interstate commerce in the products of child labor.

The District Court held the act unconstitutional and entered a decree enjoining its enforcement. This appeal brings the case here. . . .

The attack upon the act rests upon three propositions: first: it is not a regulation of interstate and foreign commerce; second: it contravenes the Tenth Amendment to the Constitution; third: it conflicts with the Fifth Amendment to the Constitution.

The controlling question for decision is: is it within the authority of Congress in regulating commerce among the States to prohibit the transportation in interstate commerce of manufactured goods, the product of a factory in which, within thirty days prior to their removal therefrom, children under the age of fourteen have been employed or permitted to work, or children between the ages of fourteen and sixteen years have been employed or permitted to work more than eight hours in any day, or more than six days in any week, or after the hour of seven o'clock P.M. or before the hour of six o'clock A.M.?

The power essential to the passage of this act, the Government contends, is found in the commerce clause of the Constitution, which authorizes Congress to regulate commerce with foreign nations and among the States.

A young girl operates a cotton mill spinning machine. In Hammer v. Dagenhart, *a suit filed by the father of two child cotton mill workers, the US Supreme Court ruled that the federal government does not have the power to regulate interstate commerce produced by child labor.* © Bettmann/Corbis/AP Images.

Past Court Cases Concerning Regulation of Interstate Commerce

In *Gibbons v. Ogden*, Chief Justice [John] Marshall, speaking for this court and defining the extent and nature of the commerce power, said, "It is the power to regulate; that is, to prescribe the rule by which commerce is to be governed." In other words, the power is one to control the means by which commerce is carried on, which is directly the contrary of the assumed right to forbid commerce from moving, and thus destroy it as to particular commodities. But it is insisted that adjudged cases in this court establish the doctrine that the power to regulate given to Congress incidentally includes the authority to prohibit the movement of ordinary commodities, and therefore that the subject is not open for discussion. The cases demonstrate the contrary. They rest upon the character of the particular subjects dealt with, and the fact that the scope of governmental authority, state or national, possessed over them is such that the authority to prohibit is as to them but the exertion of the power to regulate.

The first of these cases is *Champion v. Ames*, the so-called *Lottery Case*, in which it was held that Congress might pass a law having the effect to keep the channels of commerce free from use in the transportation of tickets used in the promotion of lottery schemes. In *Hipolite Egg Co. v. United States*, this court sustained the power of Congress to pass the Pure Food and Drug Act, which prohibited the introduction into the States by means of interstate commerce of impure foods and drugs. In *Hoke v. United States,* this court sustained the constitutionality of the so-called "White Slave Traffic Act," whereby the transportation of a woman in interstate commerce for the purpose of prostitution was forbidden. In that case, we said, having reference to the authority of Congress, under the regulatory power, to protect the channels of interstate commerce:

> "If the facility of interstate transportation can be taken away from the demoralization of lotteries, the debasement of obscene literature, the contagion of diseased cattle or persons, the impurity of food and drugs, the like facility can be taken away from the systematic enticement to and the enslavement in prostitution and debauchery of women, and, more insistently, of girls."

In *Caminetti v. United States,* we held that Congress might prohibit the transportation of women in interstate commerce for the purposes of debauchery and kindred purposes. In *Clark Distilling Co. v. Western Maryland Ry. Co.,* the power of Congress over the transportation of intoxicating liquors was sustained. In the course of the opinion, it was said:

> "The power conferred is to regulate, and the very terms of the grant would seem to repel the contention that only prohibi-

tion of movement in interstate commerce was embraced. And the cogency of this is manifest, since, if the doctrine were applied to those manifold and important subjects of interstate commerce as to which Congress from the beginning has regulated, not prohibited, the existence of government under the Constitution would be no longer possible."

And, concluding the discussion which sustained the authority of the Government to prohibit the transportation of liquor in interstate commerce, the court said:

"... the exceptional nature of the subject here regulated is the basis upon which the exceptional power exerted must rest, and affords no ground for any fear that such power may be constitutionally extended to things which it may not, consistently with the guarantees of the Constitution, embrace."

In each of these instances, the use of interstate transportation was necessary to the accomplishment of harmful results. In other words, although the power over interstate transportation was to regulate, that could only be accomplished by prohibiting the use of the facilities of interstate commerce to effect the evil intended.

Manufacturing Is Not Commerce

This element is wanting in the present case. The thing intended to be accomplished by this statute is the denial of the facilities of interstate commerce to those manufacturers in the States who employ children within the prohibited ages. The act, in its effect, does not regulate transportation among the States, but aims to standardize the ages at which children may be employed in mining and manufacturing within the States. The goods shipped are, of themselves, harmless. The act permits them to be freely shipped after thirty days from the time of their removal from the factory. When offered for shipment, and before transportation begins, the labor of their production is over, and the mere fact that they were intended for interstate commerce transportation does not make their production subject to federal control under the commerce power.

Commerce "consists of intercourse and traffic, and includes the transportation of persons land property, as well as the purchase, sale and exchange of commodities."

The making of goods and the mining of coal are not commerce, nor does the fact that these things are to be afterwards shipped or used in interstate commerce make their production a part thereof. *Delaware, Lackawanna & Western R.R. Co. v. Yurkonis.*

Over interstate transportation or its incidents, the regulatory power of Congress is ample, but the production of articles intended for interstate commerce is a matter of local regulation. "When the commerce begins is determined not by the character of the commodity, nor by the intention of the owner to transfer it to another state for sale, nor by his preparation of it for transportation, but by its actual delivery to a common carrier for transportation, or the actual commencement of its transfer to another state." (Mr. Justice Jackson in [petition to the Supreme Court of Ohio] *In re Green.*) This principle has been recognized often in this court. *Coe v. Errol, Bacon v. Illinois*, and cases cited. If it were otherwise, all manufacture intended for interstate shipment would be brought under federal control to the practical exclusion of the authority of the States, a result certainly not contemplated by the framers of the Constitution when they vested in Congress the authority to regulate commerce among the States.

Congress Has No Power to Regulate Unfair Competition

It is further contended that the authority of Congress may be exerted to control interstate commerce in the shipment of child-made goods because of the effect of the circulation of such goods in other States where the evil of this class of labor has been recognized by local legislation, and the right to thus employ child labor has been more rigorously restrained than in the State of production. In other words, that the unfair competition thus engendered may be controlled by closing the channels of interstate commerce to manufacturers in those States where the local laws do not meet what Congress deems to be the more just standard of other States.

There is no power vested in Congress to require the States to exercise their police power so as to prevent possible unfair competition. Many causes may cooperate to give one State, by reason of local laws or conditions, an economic advantage over others. The Commerce Clause was not intended to give to Congress a general authority to equalize such conditions. In some of the States, laws have been passed fixing minimum wages for women, in others, the local law regulates the hours of labor of women in various employments. Business done in such States may be at an economic disadvantage when compared with States which have no such regulations; surely, this fact does not give Congress the power to deny transportation in interstate commerce to those who carry on business where the hours of labor and the rate of compensation for women have not been fixed by a standard in use in other States and approved by Congress.

The grant of power to Congress over the subject of interstate commerce was to enable it to regulate such commerce, and not to give it authority to control the States in their exercise of the police power over local trade and manufacture.

The grant of authority over a purely federal matter was not intended to destroy the local power always existing and carefully reserved to the States in the Tenth Amendment to the Constitution.

Police regulations relating to the internal trade and affairs of the States have been uniformly recognized as within such control. "This," said this court in *United States v. Dewitt*, "has been so frequently declared by this court, results so obviously from the terms of the Constitution, and has been so fully explained and supported on former occasions that we think it unnecessary to enter again upon the discussion."

Excerpt from the Keating-Owen Act of 1916

Be it enacted by the Senate and House of Representatives of the United States of America in Congress assembled, That no producer, manufacturer, or dealer shall ship or deliver for shipment in interstate or foreign commerce, any article or commodity the product of any mine or quarry situated in the United States, in which within thirty days prior to the time of the removal of such product therefrom children under the age of sixteen years have been employed or permitted to work, or any article or commodity the product of any mill, cannery, workshop, factory, or manufacturing establishment, situated in the United States, in which within thirty days prior to the removal of such product therefrom children under the age of fourteen years have been employed or permitted to work, or children between the ages of fourteen years and sixteen years have been employed or permitted to work more than eight hours in any day, or more than six days in any week, or after the hour of seven o'clock postmeridian, or before the hour of six o'clock antemeridian.

Keating-Owen Child Labor Act of 1916.
www.ourdocuments.gov.

The States Retain the Majority of Commerce Regulations

In the judgment which established the broad power of Congress over interstate commerce, Chief Justice Marshall said:

"They [inspection laws] act upon the subject before it becomes an article of foreign commerce, or of commerce among the states, and prepare it for that purpose. They form a portion of that immense mass of legislation which embraces everything within the territory of a state not surrendered to the general government, all which can be most advantageously exercised by the states themselves. Inspection laws, quarantine laws, health laws of every description, as well as laws for regulating the internal commerce of a state and those which respect turnpike roads, ferries, &c., are component parts of this mass."

And in *Dartmouth College v. Woodward*, the same great judge said:

> "That the framers of the constitution did not intend to restrain the states in the regulation of their civil institutions, adopted for internal government, and that the instrument they have given us is not to be so construed may be admitted."

That there should be limitations upon the right to employ children in mines and factories in the interest of their own and the public welfare, all will admit. That such employment is generally deemed to require regulation is shown by the fact that the brief of counsel states that every State in the Union has a law upon the subject, limiting the right to thus employ children. In North Carolina, the State wherein is located the factory in which the employment was had in the present case, no child under twelve years of age is permitted to work.

It may be desirable that such laws be uniform, but our Federal Government is one of enumerated powers; "this principle," declared Chief Justice Marshall in *McCulloch v. Maryland*, "is universally admitted." . . .

In interpreting the Constitution, it must never be forgotten that the Nation is made up of States to which are entrusted the powers of local government. And to them and to the people the powers not expressly delegated to the National Government are reserved. The power of the States to regulate their purely internal affairs by such laws as seem wise to the local authority is inherent, and has never been surrendered to the general government.

To sustain this statute would not be, in our judgment, a recognition of the lawful exertion of congressional authority over interstate commerce, but would sanction an invasion by the federal power of the control of a matter purely local in its character, and over which no authority has been delegated to Congress in conferring the power to regulate commerce among the States.

We have neither authority nor disposition to question the motives of Congress in enacting this legislation. The purposes intended must be attained consistently with constitutional limitations, and not by an invasion of the powers of the States. This court has no more important function than that which devolves upon it the obligation to preserve inviolate the constitutional limitations upon the exercise of authority, federal and state, to the end that each may continue to discharge, harmoniously with the other, the duties entrusted to it by the Constitution.

In our view, the necessary effect of this act is, by means of a prohibition against the movement in interstate commerce of ordinary commercial commodities, to regulate the hours of labor of children in factories and mines within the States, a purely state authority. Thus, the act in a two-fold sense is repugnant to the Constitution. It not only transcends the authority delegated to Congress over commerce, but also exerts a power as to a purely local matter to which the federal authority does not extend. The far-reaching result of upholding the act cannot be more plainly indicated than by pointing out that, if Congress can thus regulate matters entrusted to local authority by prohibition of the movement of commodities in interstate commerce, all freedom of commerce will be at an end, and the power of the States over local matters may be eliminated, and, thus, our system of government be practically destroyed.

> *"If there is any matter upon which civilized countries have agreed . . . it is the evil of premature and excessive child labor."*

Congress Does Have the Power to Regulate Child Labor Within States

Dissenting Opinion

Oliver Wendell Holmes

In the 1918 US Supreme Court case Hammer v. Dagenhart, *the defendants argued that the US Constitution did not permit the federal government to prohibit interstate commerce of goods that were produced by child labor. Five of the nine justices upheld this view, leading to a victory for the states and their industries. However, four of the justices, led by Oliver Wendell Holmes, rejected this conclusion. In the following viewpoint, Holmes claims that the judiciary has already ruled in many cases involving the regulation of interstate commerce that the US Congress's authority trumps state powers in cross-border trade. Though the defendants charged that this Congressional control extends only to the goods and not the means of production, Holmes dismisses this contention by asserting that Congress's power is broad and far reaching as long as the manufactured goods are moved across state lines. He maintains that Congress and the Supreme Court have already weighed in on the prohibition of lottery fraud; therefore the "evil" of child labor is surely within the discretionary powers of the federal government. Though Holmes's argument did not change the opinion of the court in 1918, it was cited in the 1941 Supreme Court case* United States v. Darby Lumber Co., *which overturned the* Hammer *ruling and reasserted Congress's power to regulate all aspects of interstate commerce.*

The single question in this case is whether Congress has power to prohibit the shipment in interstate or foreign commerce of any product of a cotton mill situated in the United States in which, within thirty days before the removal of the product, children under fourteen have been employed or children between fourteen and sixteen have been employed more than eight hours in a day, or more than six days in any week, or between seven in the evening and six in the morning. The objection urged against the power is that the States have exclusive control over their methods of production, and that Congress cannot meddle with them, and, taking the proposition in the sense of direct intermeddling, I agree to it, and suppose that no one denies it. But if an act is within the powers specifically conferred upon Congress, it seems to me that it is not made any less constitutional because of the indirect effects that it may have, however obvious it may be that it will have those effects, and that we are not at liberty upon such grounds to hold it void.

Congress Has the Power to Regulate Interstate Trade

The first step in my argument is to make plain what no one is likely to dispute—that the statute in question is within the power expressly given to Congress if considered only as to its immediate effects, and that, if invalid, it is so only upon some collateral

1920 CENSUS DATA ON CHILD LABOR IN THE UNITED STATES

The 1920 US Census discovered 1.06 million children between the ages of 10 and 15 who were "gainfully employed" or who "contributed materially" to the family income. (The total population for that age group was 12.5 million.) Of this million plus, 714,000 were boys and 346,000 were girls. More than 60 percent—647,000—were engaged in agriculture. The rest worked as or in:

		% of Total Employed
Messenger & office boys/girls	48,028	11.6
Servants/waiters	41,586	10.1
Sales	30,370	7.3
Clerks	22,521	5.4
Cotton-mill operatives	21,875	5.3
Newsboys	20,706	5.0
Iron/steel industry operatives	12,904	3.1
Clothing industry operatives	11,757	2.8
Lumber/furniture industry operatives	10,585	2.6
Silk-mill operatives	10,023	2.4
Shoe factory operatives	7,545	1.8
Woolen-worsted machine operatives	7,077	1.7
Coal mine operatives	5,850	1.4
All other occupations	162,722	39.3

Taken from: Bill Kaufman, "The Child Labor Amendment Debate of the 1920s," *Essays in Political Economy*, November 1992.

ground. The statute confines itself to prohibiting the carriage of certain goods in interstate or foreign commerce. Congress is given power to regulate such commerce in unqualified terms. It would not be argued today that the power to regulate does not include the power to prohibit. Regulation means the prohibition of something, and when interstate commerce is the matter to be regulated, I cannot doubt that the regulation may prohibit any part of such commerce that Congress sees fit to forbid. At all events, it is established by the *Lottery Case* and others that have followed it that a law is not beyond the regulative power of Congress merely because it prohibits certain transportation out and out. So I repeat that this statute, in its immediate operation, is clearly within the Congress' constitutional power.

The question, then, is narrowed to whether the exercise of its otherwise constitutional power by Congress can be pronounced unconstitutional because of its possible reaction upon the conduct of the States in a matter upon which I have admitted that they are free from direct control. I should have thought that that matter had been disposed of so fully as to leave no room for doubt. I should have thought that the most conspicuous decisions of this Court had made it clear that the power to regulate commerce and other constitutional powers could not be cut down or qualified by the fact that it might interfere with the carrying out of the domestic policy of any State.

The Judiciary Has Always Upheld Congress's Right to Regulate Commerce

The manufacture of oleomargarine is as much a matter of state regulation as the manufacture of cotton cloth. Congress levied a tax upon the compound when colored so as to resemble butter that was so great as obviously to prohibit the manufacture and sale. In a very elaborate discussion, the present Chief Justice [Edward D. White, who voted with the majority in *Hammer v. Dagenhart*] excluded any inquiry into the purpose of an act which, apart from that purpose, was within the power of Congress. . . . Fifty years ago, a tax on state banks the obvious purpose and actual effect of which was to drive them, or at least their circulation, out of existence was sustained although the result was one that Congress had no constitutional power to require. [In *Veazie Bank v. Fenno*] The Court made short work of the argument as to the purpose of the act. "The judicial cannot prescribe to the legislative department of the government limitations upon the exercise of its acknowledged powers." So it well might have been argued that the corporation tax was intended, under the guise of a revenue measure, to secure a control not otherwise belonging to Congress, but the tax was sustained, and the objection, so far as noticed, was disposed of by citing *McCray v. United States. Flint v. Stone Tracy Co.* And to come to cases upon interstate commerce, notwithstanding *United States v. E.C. Knight Co.*, the Sherman Act has been made an instrument for the breaking up of combinations in restraint of trade and monopolies, using the power to regulate commerce as a foothold, but not proceeding because that commerce was the end actually in mind. The objection that the control of the States over production was interfered with was urged again and again, but always in vain. . . . The Pure Food and Drug Act which was sustained in *Hipolite Egg Co. v. United States*, with the intimation that "no trade can be carried on between the States to which it [the power of Congress to regulate commerce] does not extend," applies not merely to articles that the changing opinions of the time condemn as intrinsically harmful, but to others innocent in themselves, simply on the ground that the order for them was induced by a preliminary fraud. It does not matter whether the supposed evil precedes or follows the transportation. It is enough that, in the opinion of Congress, the transportation encourages the evil. I may add that, in the cases on the so-called White Slave Act, it was established that the means adopted by Congress as convenient to the exercise of its power might have the character of police regulations. In *Clark Distilling Co. v. Western Maryland Ry. Co.* [and] *Leisy v.*

US Supreme Court Justice Oliver Wendell Holmes opposed the ruling in Hammer v. Dagenhart, *asserting that the US Congress has the power to regulate interstate commerce produced by child labor.* © Getty Images.

Hardin, is quoted with seeming approval to the effect that "a subject matter which has been confided exclusively to Congress by the Constitution is not within the jurisdiction of the police power of the State unless placed there by congressional action. I see no reason for that proposition not applying here."

State Power Ends at the State Border

The notion that prohibition is any less prohibition when applied to things now thought evil I do not understand. But if there is any matter upon which civilized countries have agreed—far more unanimously than they have with regard to intoxicants and some other matters over which this country is now emotionally aroused—it is the evil of premature and excessive child labor. I should have thought that, if we were to introduce our own moral conceptions where in my opinion they do not belong, this was preeminently a case for upholding the exercise of all its powers by the United States.

But I had thought that the propriety of the exercise of a power admitted to exist in some cases was for the consideration of Congress alone, and that this Court always had disavowed the right to intrude its judgment upon questions of policy or morals. It is not for this Court to pronounce when prohibition is necessary to regulation—if it ever may be necessary—to say that it is permissible as against strong drink, but not as against the product of ruined lives.

The act does not meddle with anything belonging to the States. They may regulate their internal affairs and their domestic commerce as they like. But when they seek to send their products across the state line, they are no longer within their rights. If there were no Constitution and no Congress, their power to cross the line would depend upon their neighbors. Under the Constitution, such commerce belongs not to the States, but to Congress to regulate. It may carry out its views of public policy whatever indirect effect they may have upon the activities of the States. Instead of being encountered by a prohibitive tariff at her boundaries, the State encounters the public policy of the United States, which it is for Congress to express. The public policy of the United States is shaped with a view to the benefit of the nation as a whole. If, as has been the case within the memory of men still living, a State should take a different view of the propriety of sustaining a lottery from that which generally prevails, I cannot believe that the fact would require a different decision from that reached in *Champion v. Ames*. Yet, in that case, it would be said with quite as much force as in this that Congress was attempting to intermeddle with the State's domestic affairs. The national welfare, as understood by Congress, may require a different attitude within its sphere from that of some self-seeking State. It seems to me entirely constitutional for Congress to enforce its understanding by all the means at its command.

> *"If we [want to abolish child labor],*
> *then every reasonable law to that*
> *end—whether federal or state—should*
> *be approved by decent people."*

Congress Should Adopt a Child Labor Amendment

Arthur Garfield Hays

In 1924, federal legislators first proposed a Child Labor Amendment to the US Constitution that sought to vest Congress with the express power to regulate the labor of persons under eighteen years of age. The amendment passed Congress and was ratified by twenty-eight states, but its conditions could not take effect until more states adopted it. Subsequent attempts to jumpstart the stalled amendment met with failed progress. In 1935, the amendment reappeared in the national forum, and advocates and critics voiced their opinions in public. Arthur Garfield Hays, a New York lawyer and civil liberties champion, delivered a radio speech in which he pushed for adoption of the amendment. The following viewpoint is the text of that speech, in which Hays dismisses arguments of opponents as being motivated by a desire to continue the enslavement of the weak.

A few days ago I remarked to a friend of mine that I was debating over the radio on the question of the passage of the Child Labor Amendment. Answered the friend, "You don't mean to say that anyone opposes it?" "Yes," I replied, "my particular opponent is Merwin K. Hart, who represents the New York State Economic Council, which I am informed is an organization of employers. The National Manufacturers Association has been against the bill from the very beginning. That is not surprising; the amazing thing, however, is that people of great sympathy, of broad understanding are likewise opposed to the bill." "That's horrible," said my friend, "You don't mean to say that they believe that child labor should be permitted?" "No," I answered, "probably some of them do, but even they don't admit it. Occasionally one hears of the God-given right of children to work and the 'corrupting morass of idleness.' At the beginnings of the factory system we heard of the God-given right even of babies to work. We heard of the God-given right of parents to use their children to add to the family income. Yet everyone knows that this God-given right is a curse of poverty. It is wrong to designate a necessity as a right. Sometimes the right of the child to work is a correlative of the right of the adult to starve." "Well," said my friend, "what do these people contend?"

I answered that at the hearing in Albany the other day the Federal Child Labor Amendment was designated as a scheme of Communistic Russia, as an indication of a desire to nationalize children. This sounds like the laugh of the week—but it is seriously suggested.

The Persistence of a National Problem

The workings of the human mind are amazing. For a hundred years we have been trying to abolish child labor in this country. The problem is a national one for, so long as we have a system of competition, the meanest employer—who hires the cheapest labor, even to the extent of exploiting children—has the advantage over the decent man, a situation which it was thought the N.R.A.

Famed Reformer Florence Kelley Calls upon Congress to Pass a Child Labor Amendment

It is a very difficult task that confronts the Congress to draft an amendment which will find ratification quickly in the States, which will meet the difficulties which can be raised theoretically in amending the Constitution, and will do the thing that the times call for. But what is easiest to overlook, I think, at any time under an act of expediency, is the claim of the children who will so soon stand where we now stand, and who will so soon be the republic.

I think the thing easiest to sacrifice, easiest to compromise away, easiest to overlook is the claim of the children that as great care, as much time, and as open a mind with regard to the future shall be given in their behalf as in behalf of any interest or any group of people whoever claimed the attention of Congress.

Florence Kelley, National Consumers' League statement, Hearings Before Sub-Committee of Senate Committee on the Judiciary, January 1923.

[National Recovery Administration, a New Deal organization charged with establishing fair labor standards] would correct. Thus we find that between 1920 and 1930, although the number of children under sixteen years of age employed in the textile industry in the United States decreased by almost sixty per cent, yet the number of children employed in such establishments in South Carolina and Georgia increased 23 per cent and 12 per cent, respectively, during the same period. Each state fears to take any step to abolish child labor alone and thus to subject its industries to competition with states which still permit cheap children to be employed. As recently as 1933, when unemployment was at its peak, bills to raise to sixteen years the age for full-time employment were introduced in eleven states and rejected in all but two. And yet a few months later when sixteen years was established as a minimum age for employment on a national basis through the industrial codes, this was acclaimed everywhere by industry. As President [Franklin D.] Roosevelt said:

> One of the accomplishments under the National Recovery Act which has given me the greatest gratification is the outlawing of child labor. It shows how simple a long-desired reform, which no individual or state could accomplish alone, may be brought about when people work together. It is my desire that the advances attained through the National Recovery Act be made permanent. In the child labor field the obvious method of maintaining the present gains is through ratification of the Child Labor Amendment. I hope this may be achieved.

The absurdity of the arguments of people who regard all social legislation as communistic and thus seek to damn such progressive measures by a label, is indicated by the fact that this amendment was drafted, among others, by ex-Senator Thomas J. Walsh, of Montana, and George Wharton Pepper, of Pennsylvania; that in the Senate it was supported by Henry Cabot Lodge, Republican leader, and Joseph T. Robinson, Democratic leader; that among its sponsors were the American Federation of Labor, the American Association of Social Workers, the American Federation of Teachers, Federal Council of the Churches of Christ, the Railroad Brotherhoods, and even the Young Women's Christian Association and the National Women's Christian Temperance Union. Never before have such organizations been regarded as radical.

Fears of Potential Congressional Abuse

Since few people care to argue that child labor should be permitted, the objection is made to a national amendment rather than to the purposes which that amendment seeks to accomplish. The amendment gives Congress the power to limit, regulate and prohibit the labor of persons under eighteen years of age. It is not a statute; it does not contain the details but merely gives general power to pass legislation. In this respect it differs from the Eighteenth Amendment, the failure of which can be largely attributed to the fact that the amendment itself prohibited the manufacture, sale and transportation of alcoholic beverages. It did not limit itself to giving Congress the power to pass legislation; it contained an absolute prohibition.

This amendment gives Congress the power; the fears as to what might result from this amendment are due to the assumption that Congress would abuse the power. Likewise there must be the assumption that if the power were left with the states—where it is now—they would not abuse it. Now, Congress may not always be wise any more than state legislators are wise, but the very basis of representative government necessitates taking the chance on legislative bodies exercising some intelligent discretion.

We would have an army of snoopers and investigators, say the opponents. They will exercise supervision and control over every family in the United States. Why the assumption? As a matter of fact we have had child labor laws passed by Congress on two different occasions. Both were declared unconstitutional by divided court opinion. The first Federal Child Labor law carried an appropriation of $150,000 for enforcement and the staff of the Child Labor Division contained fifty-one persons. The second Federal Child Labor law involved appropriations running from $88,000 to $130,000, and the personnel was about the same number as before. The Federal Government in each case worked with the State Department of Labor.

Such Fears Are Petty and Unreasonable

It is significant that according to the Seventh Annual Report of the Chief of the Children's Bureau, the effect of the decision of

Attorney Arthur Garfield Hays (center) addresses a crowd in Jersey City. Hays was a vocal advocate for the passage of the Child Labor Amendment in 1935. © Bettmann/Corbis/AP Images.

the Supreme Court in states where the state child labor standards were lower than those imposed by the federal law, was a prompt restoration of the longer working day for children under sixteen and an increase in the number of such children. There was likewise an appreciable increase in the violation of state laws.

But the opponents of the law get legalistic. Our great manufacturers have all become jurists. This amendment gives Congress the power to do all sorts of things, and look what might happen if they exercised that power! This suggestion seems ludicrous in view of the fact that Congress today has the power to confiscate our property through tax laws, to put us into war, to place us on the firing line, and practically to dispose of the lives and liberty of all of us. Somehow or other I cannot feel that the power to limit or prohibit child labor is as serious as these powers that Congress already has. If I must perforce leave these other powers with Congress, I am not worried about Congress having power over child labor. As Senator Walsh once pointed out, Congress has power to make treaties. The Senate and the President of the United States could cede Montana and attach it to the Dominion of Canada, but, as he said, "are we going to deny to the Senate and to the President of the United States the power to make treaties because, forsooth, they may make treaties which would be destructive of the integrity of the United States?"

But, say the opponents, this will indirectly give Congress the power to control education. It does not say so. The powers not expressly delegated to the United States remain with the states. It is an absurd use of words to suggest that a power to control labor involves the power to control education. Words are used in the law with some reference to the ends intended to be accomplished. As Judge [Oliver Wendell] Holmes once said:

> A word is not a crystal, transparent and unchanged. It is the skin of a living thought and may vary greatly in color and content according to the circumstances and the time in which it is used.

Everyone knows what is meant by labor. It has to do with physical labor in this amendment. The same question arose under the Contract Labor laws, but it was there held that a minister was not subject to its provisions, or a chemist, or other professional men. It might be argued that laws against Sunday labor would apply to reading the newspapers, to playing golf, to listening to the radio, or even to going to church. But nobody would be so foolish as to claim that that was intended.

"But," say our opponents, "why eighteen years of age? Many youths are quite capable of helping support the family before that time. This might prevent home chores of boys on the farm, or the assistance of the young women in housework." Again it is overlooked that the amendment merely gives power to make laws. It is hardly to be assumed that Congress would necessarily make fool laws to prevent the kind of work to which nobody objects. As Henry A. Wallace, Secretary of Agriculture, recently stated:

> Coming from an agricultural state, I am familiar with the attempts of opponents of the amendment to arouse employers against it on the ground that farm boys and girls would no longer [be] permitted to help with the chores and that the parents' authority over their children would be seriously impaired. Of course this is nonsense and every fair-minded person who knows anything at all about the proposed amendment knows that it is nonsense.

Time to End the Exploitation of the Weak

One could continue *ad nauseam* with these legalistic arguments. A contention is made that since the amendment was proposed ten years ago and has not yet been ratified, that it cannot legally become a part of the Constitution at this late date. Argument is made that since some states refused to ratify it on one occasion, they no longer may ratify it. If the amendment cannot legally be made a part of the Constitution at this late date, I am wondering why these eminent lawyers worry about its ratification.

Substantially the same kind of argument as is made here has been made against every piece of social legislation, whether state or national which has tended toward social betterment. I have in mind the eight-hour day, workmen's compensation laws, minimum wage laws and legislation of like kind. The same kind of people are usually lined up on the opposing side. I'll venture the opinion that without exception the opponents of this amendment are opposed to Section 7-a of the National Industrial Recovery Act [which protected the collective bargaining rights of unions].

What these people object to is social legislation. They object to the endeavor to improve conditions by preventing the strong from exploiting the weak. The argument is usually based upon the God-given right of people to ruin themselves and their children—the freedom to contract to become slaves. The arguments are always placed upon different grounds. Substantially the question is whether we want to get rid of child labor in this country. If we do, then every reasonable law to that end—whether federal or state—should be approved by decent people.

> *"The leadership of the future will be founded on commercial and industrial progress. . . . The constitutionality of such legislation [will allow] Congress to shackle commerce and strangle industry."*

Congress Should Not Adopt a Child Labor Amendment

Duncan U. Fletcher

In the following viewpoint, Duncan U. Fletcher speaks out against the passage of a proposed Child Labor Amendment that would reach congressional consideration in 1924. Fletcher rejects the amendment, insisting that the states have the ultimate power to control child labor within their borders. He maintains that the states already have laws in place to regulate working ages and adding an extra level of federal oversight would be unnecessary and intrusive. Believing that regulations should fit the needs of the community, Fletcher claims that in some instances child labor is a needed and beneficial contribution. Fletcher was the longest serving US senator in Florida's history (1909–1936).

Clearly the States have the power and authority to deal with the subject of child labor in all its phases. There is no dispute as to that and the States are dealing with it. Many, if not all States, have laws that declare no child under 16 years of age shall be employed in any occupation injurious to health or dangerous to life, limb, or the morals of such child.

No Need for Federal Oversight

Florida provides a State inspector, whose duty it is to see to the enforcement of the law. I know of no complaint in that regard. I deny that there is need of Federal inspectors to supervise the work of State officers, empowered to harass and inconvenience and oppress our people by arbitrary inspections, making complaints before United States commissioners, arresting and prosecuting them before the Federal courts in the process of earning their salaries. We have too many inspectors, special agents, secret service employees, and the like now, costing the people hundreds of thousands of dollars for the privilege of being watched from the time they arise in the morning until they retire at night.

Laws have been and are being enacted by the States on this subject, as fast and as effective as the need for them is brought home to the people. Local conditions should not be ignored, and these conditions no general national legislation can adequately meet. Granted such legislation proposed would serve a high purpose, I cannot believe it would be wise to pass Federal legislation or that it is the best way to handle the subject. It is a field already occupied by practically all the States, and the States and local communities are in position to deal with it directly and to correct every evil, national or individual, which it is desired to correct.

Undermining Commerce and Constitutional Liberties

It is argued that the State laws are not enforced, but I answer, who is given the right to pass that judgment, and if that conclusion be true, it by no means follows the Congress has power for that reason to go into a State and interpose to correct such dereliction. That would be an unwarranted, bold assumption of power by Congress.

US Senator Duncan U. Fletcher argued that child workers—such as these young shoe shiners— can benefit society. Fletcher opposed the passage of the Child Labor Amendment in 1924. © Lewis W. Hine/Buyenlarge/Getty Images.

I can quite appreciate that in some circumstances and under some conditions the privilege of a child under 16, and even under 14, years of age to work is a blessing of the highest character. The welfare of the child, the good of society, may be subserved by the reasonable employment of such a child in useful labor. Work, under proper conditions—wholesome, healthful employment, not too hard or difficult—never on earth injuriously affected the morals of the child. Idleness, with its proximate consequences, on the other hand, voluntary or forced, has always been a fruitful source of vice and evil.

The situation does not make it necessary or justify the enactment by Congress, in the public interest, of a measure which must inevitably lead to conflict of jurisdiction, confusion of laws, and clashing of authority. Such legislation would open the way, move far along that road which leads toward the gradual destruction of the rights of the States and the undermining of the constitutional

STATES WITH A MINIMUM WORKING AGE OF 14 IN FACTORIES AND CANNERIES, 1923

Up to This Standard or Higher

Alabama	Montana	Oregon
Connecticut	Nebraska	Pennsylvania
Florida	New Hampshire	Rhode Island
Illinois	New York	South Carolina
Indiana	North Dakota	Tennessee
Kansas	Ohio (employment	West Virginia
Kentucky	in "irregular service"	Wisconsin
Louisiana	permitted under 14	
Maine	outside school hours,	
Maryland	but this must not be	
Massachusetts	in work forbidden	
Michigan	by any Federal law)	
Minnesota	Oklahoma	

Up to This Standard with Exceptions

Arizona	Idaho	North Carolina
Arkansas	Iowa	South Dakota
California	Missouri	Texas
Colorado	Nevada	Vermont
District of Columbia	New Jersey	Washington
Georgia	New Mexico	

Below This Standard

Delaware (12 in canneries; also other exemptions)

Mississippi (boy 12, girl 14; penalty clause omits canneries)

Utah (no minimum age except in certain dangerous occupations)

Virginia (12 in canneries in vacation and outside school hours)

Wyoming (no minimum age except in certain dangerous occupations)

Taken from: US Children's Bureau, "Present Status of Child Labor Laws in the States," *Congressional Digest*, February 1923.

liberty Americans have not ceased to love. The leadership of the future will be founded on commercial and industrial progress. Admit the constitutionality of such legislation and you recognize a power in Congress to shackle commerce and strangle industry. When that day comes you will realize you have thrown to the winds the leadership and the power of the United States.

| "If teenagers find happiness in challenging and demanding work, then we must respect their right to pursue it."

Teenagers Have a Right to Work

V. Nathaniel Ang

While the Fair Labor Standards Act was instrumental in prohibiting young people from exploitation in the workplace, some critics have charged that it has resulted in US youth opting out of the valuable pursuit of employment. In the following viewpoint, V. Nathaniel Ang argues that teenagers have a fundamental right to work outlined in both the Declaration of Independence and the Bill of Rights. He believes the law should recognize this right and permit teenagers emancipation to hold any job they choose. Ang bases his argument on the notion that employment benefits the teenager by making them productive citizens and aids communities that have a need for low-cost labor. Ang, an associate lawyer in Texas, wrote the following viewpoint when he was a law student at the University of Pennsylvania.

V. Nathaniel Ang, "Teenage Employment Emancipation and the Law," *University of Pennsylvania Journal of Labor and Employment*, Winter 2007, pp. 389–419. Copyright © 2007 by University of Pennsylvania Law School. All rights reserved. Reproduced by permission.

If teenagers have a right to gainful employment, then this right can be found in the Declaration of Independence and the Ninth Amendment. The Declaration of Independence offers a robust libertarian argument for teenagers' right to seek gainful employment: "We hold these truths to be self-evident, that all men are created equal, that they are endowed by their Creator with certain unalienable Rights, that among these are Life, Liberty and the pursuit of Happiness."

Pursuing Happiness Through Work

The Founding Fathers did not define "pursuit of happiness" but assumed that common sense would be sufficient to define it. It might be helpful to turn to some natural law theorists and see how they defined the "pursuit of happiness." According to [seventeenth-century English philosopher] John Locke, happiness is "the utmost pleasure we are capable of." According to [eighteenth-century Swiss legal theorist] Jean Jacques Burlamaqui, "By *Happiness* we are to understand the internal satisfaction of the mind, arising from the possession of good: and by good whatever is suitable or agreeable to man for his preservation, perfection, conveniency, or pleasure." Therefore, the "pursuit of happiness" probably means the pursuit of good, or the pursuit of pleasure. Happiness comes in different forms for each person, but every person has the right to pursue happiness.

In my opinion, the "pursuit of happiness" has a special meaning for teenagers. Teenagerhood is a time of transition when young people start to acquire the privileges and responsibilities of adulthood. Hence, the "pursuit of happiness" presumes that teenagers have the prerogative of acting like adults and being treated like adults, if conducive to their happiness. Teenagers may find happiness in any of several vocations, including higher education, sports, community service, or work. If teenagers find happiness in challenging and demanding work, then we must respect their right to pursue it.

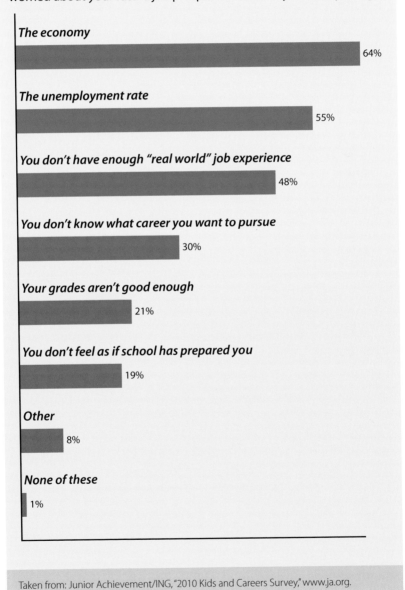

LACK OF JOB EXPERIENCE IS AMONG TEENS' FEARS CONCERNING JOB PROSPECTS

Which, if any, of the following are reasons why you might feel more worried about your future job prospects now than you felt a year ago?

The economy
64%

The unemployment rate
55%

You don't have enough "real world" job experience
48%

You don't know what career you want to pursue
30%

Your grades aren't good enough
21%

You don't feel as if school has prepared you
19%

Other
8%

None of these
1%

Taken from: Junior Achievement/ING, "2010 Kids and Careers Survey," www.ja.org.

Ninth Amendment Rights

Furthermore, the Bill of Rights implicitly recognizes teenagers' employment rights: "The enumeration in the Constitution, of certain rights, shall not be construed to deny or disparage others retained by the people." Employment rights are not expressly articulated anywhere in the Constitution, but they are encompassed within the Ninth Amendment. In *Richmond Newspapers, Inc. v. Virginia*, the Supreme Court explained the purpose of the Ninth Amendment by examining its legislative history. When the Bill of Rights was proposed in Congress, many legislators foresaw that some rights would be left unmentioned and feared that these rights would not be recognized by the government. James Madison assuaged their fears by claiming that the proposed Ninth Amendment would serve to guard against the denial of certain rights that were not specifically mentioned in the Constitution. Consequently, being that work is so important and necessary to human life, the right to gainful employment must fall within the protection of the Ninth Amendment, even though it is not expressly articulated anywhere in the Constitution.

A Fundamental Human Right

The right to seek gainful employment is a fundamental human right for at least three reasons. First, work is a means of meeting basic human needs. Second, work is a means of acquiring private property. Third, work allows individuals to achieve their full human potential. Because work is important and necessary for human life, the right to seek gainful employment must exist as a self-evident fact, and it is protected by the Ninth Amendment.

Teenagers are human beings, too. Therefore, it is only reasonable to start recognizing teenagers' employment rights. In much of human history, most teenagers were considered adults. It was only in the last hundred years or so that society started treating teenagers differently.

Admittedly, employment rights are not absolute; governments can place limits on the exercise of employment rights. In order to protect the public welfare, governments have the power to pass child labor laws. However, child labor laws should not come at the expense of teenagers' employment rights. The line between childhood and teenagerhood must necessarily remain imprecise. However, for the sake of teenagers who are mature enough to take on adult responsibilities, this bar should be set lower.

Employment Makes Teenagers Productive Citizens

Working age laws are based on the presumption that teenagers are incapable of taking on important responsibilities. This functions as a self-fulfilling prophecy, to the detriment of teenagers. The denial of employment rights serves as a denial of the opportunity to take on real responsibilities and gain beneficial learning experience. Teenagers in the United States have a prolonged childhood. As a consequence, they are overly pampered and take too long to mature.

Work is an effective means of achieving personal growth and maturity. Through work, teenagers learn discipline, self-reliance, and responsibility. History teaches us that work experience can make young persons more responsible and mature; George Washington, Alexander Hamilton, and Benjamin Franklin are common examples. George Washington was a surveyor at age sixteen. This was at a time when most of Virginia was still uncharted territory. His surveying commissions took him deep into the backwoods where he faced many occupational hazards. Alexander Hamilton was an artillery captain at age nineteen. On the battlefield, he was responsible for the lives of soldiers older than himself. Benjamin Franklin had his own printing business by age twenty-four. Success took years of hard work and perseverance. While still a teenager, he was already making a name in the profession.

Teenagers of today's time have less work experience and show less maturity. As one parent remarked, "I see kids watching TV.

The right of teenagers to seek employment falls under the protection of the Ninth Amendment. Some argue that working makes teenagers more productive members of society. © Comstock Images/Getty Images.

They don't know what to do with themselves. Shouldn't they be occupied doing something worthwhile?" Aside from watching too much TV, there are even worse problems: violence, alcoholism, and drug abuse are rampant among teenagers.

The relationship between teenage delinquency and teenage unemployment is complex. However, it is reasonable to say that better employment opportunities will be a step in the right direction. Employment emancipation will give teenagers an outlet for their youthful energy and encourage them to be productive citizens.

Ideally, working age restrictions are meant to encourage teenagers to finish their high school education. The law is concerned that work should not interfere with schooling—and this is a reasonable concern. However, there is a better strategy for encouraging teenagers to finish high school, namely improving education, instead of punishing teenage employment.

Moreover, the law seems to have an unreasonable anti-employment bias. In its grand desire to regulate the lives of teenagers, the law serves to frustrate their legitimate interests. The law prohibits teenagers from working in their desired occupations, thereby keeping useful skills and training out of their reach. Therefore, the law is failing our teenagers.

Teenage Employment Emancipation Is Good Public Policy

Society will benefit from teenage employment emancipation. Teenagers provide much-needed labor resources at low cost. The demand for teenage employment is significant. Hence, teenage employment should be encouraged as a matter of public policy. One public policy concern resolved by teenage employment emancipation is community need, a good example of which is the sudden upsurge of construction demand after natural disasters. Hurricane Katrina of 2005 left many Gulf Coast communities in need of immediate rebuilding. The availability of teenage workers would have expedited the rebuilding of coastal cities and towns.

Another public policy concern alleviated by teenage employment emancipation is economic hardship. The incidence of poverty among teenagers is significant. According to the U.S. Census

Bureau, the poverty rate among persons below the age of eighteen is 18.5%, which is higher than the poverty rate of 13.3% for the general population. The problem of teenage poverty can be alleviated through the employment emancipation of teenage workers from the poorest families.

> "The FLSA has not been significantly
> amended since its adoption in 1938.
> Many youth workers are not covered;
> penalties for violation of the act are
> extraordinarily lax."

Child Labor Protections Are Outdated

Seymour Moskowitz

In the following viewpoint, Seymour Moskowitz claims that legal protections for child laborers in the United States are insufficient. He asserts that the Fair Labor Standards Act (FLSA), the chief law that regulates child labor, was a product of the Great Depression when many children never finished high school and entered the workforce full-time. Today, Moskowitz writes, high school students often work and pursue an education, leaving them with different concerns and vulnerabilities. Pointing out that the FLSA has not been amended significantly since its inception, Moskowitz states that this law and various state laws have not caught up with the times and are not providing young workers with the safeguards they need. Moskowitz is a professor of law at Valparaiso University in Indiana.

Seymour Moskowitz, "Save the Children: The Legal Abandonment of American Youth in the Workplace," *Akron Law Review*, 2010, pp. 107–161.

> "[I]f there is any matter upon which civilized countries have agreed . . . it is the evil of premature and excessive child labor."

The "evil" referred to by [US Supreme Court] Justice Oliver Wendell Holmes, Jr. in his famous 1918 dissent was the effect of child labor upon minors, their families, and society in general. In the late-nineteenth and early-twentieth centuries, agricultural and industrial production in the United States included masses of children working forty or more hours per week in mines, mills, factories, and on farms. A powerful American movement arose to end child labor, led by famous progressive reformers like Jacob Riis, Jane Addams, and Florence Kelley, aided by attorney and later Supreme Court Justice Louis Brandeis. After an extraordinary crusade spanning more than three-quarters of a century, Congress passed and the Supreme Court upheld, the Fair Labor Standards Act (FLSA) that included restrictions on child labor. This long-sought legislative prize was won only after repeated Supreme Court invalidations of federal and state statutes designed to limit or outlaw child labor and an unsuccessful campaign to pass a constitutional amendment on the topic.

Child Labor Persists in America

The FLSA was enacted more than seventy years ago. Today, the mention of "child labor" brings forth nostalgic recollection of a distant struggle and the self-satisfied perception that, at least here in the United States, we have abolished this ancient evil. Tragically, this perception is only half true. With the exception of agriculture workers, minors under age 14 are in school and not engaged in paid work. Between three and five million adolescents, however, work after school; these numbers include several hundred thousand minors employed in agriculture. The United States has the highest percentage of working children of any developed nation; many children even work long hours during the school week.

Employment presents potential benefits for the adolescent, including income, valuable lessons about responsibility and fi-

Youth labor advocates argue that the Fair Labor Standards Act, enacted in 1938, does not properly safeguard teenagers working in today's labor environment. © Jamie Grill/Getty Images.

nances, and transferrable job skills. However, children's work in the United States—especially "high intensity" work, i.e., more than twenty hours per week—poses substantial immediate and long-term academic, safety, and health risks for youth workers. Adolescents with jobs, especially those working twenty or more hours, have less academic success in high school, increased absences and drop-out rates, and lower grade-point averages than those who do not work or those who work fewer hours. They are more likely to drop out or be suspended from school, use cigarettes and other harmful substances, have more traffic accidents and teenage pregnancies, and experience a wide variety of other negative outcomes. These jobs tend to weaken the social controls exerted by school and family restraining deviant behavior. Many teenagers are killed on the job and approximately 100,000 to 200,000 are injured annually.

Shortcomings of the Fair Labor Standards Act

The federal Fair Labor Standards Act and state law govern child labor in the United States. The FLSA has not been significantly amended since its adoption in 1938. Many youth workers are not covered; penalties for violation of the act are extraordinarily lax. Unlike most federal civil rights statutes, the FLSA gives no private right of action. The most affected parties—aggrieved minor employees and their parents—are unable to sue. Enforcement is left entirely to administrative processes, and it is clear that the Department of Labor's (DOL) enforcement activities—both adjudicatory and rulemaking—are inadequate. The vast majority of state child labor laws and enforcement are also woefully weak. Children are *de facto* [in fact] left without protection in the workplace, with disastrous consequences.

Youth workers are particularly vulnerable in agriculture. From its inception, the FLSA excluded farm workers. As part of the rural labor force, children were not protected by the statute. Several amendments to the federal statute provided limited coverage, but even children working in agriculture today receive dramatically less protection than those working in all other economic sectors. Hundreds of thousands of children do farm work, one of the most dangerous jobs for youths. Minor farm workers are legally permitted to work in more hazardous occupations and for longer periods of time than other minor workers. No maximum hours restrictions apply to their labor. They work before and after school; perform arduous physical labor; and risk illness, exposure to pesticides, serious injury, and permanent disability. Of work-related deaths in employees under 18, 41 percent occurred in agriculture and a staggering 20 percent were child farm workers 13 years of age or younger.

Teens Have More Freedom Today

In addition to these academic and non-academic risks of child labor in the United States, in an ironic aberration, teenagers are given remarkable legal independence in decision-making regarding work and school. In almost every other area of law, adolescents are protected from imprudent choices because of their developmental stage. Parents are entrusted with decision-making power on matters with long-term consequences. School and work choices, however, are treated in a dramatically different, laissez-faire manner. Twenty-four states set 16 as the minimum age to leave school, and seven states set the age at 17. Seventeen of these states allow 16- and 17-year-olds to withdraw from school without parental consent. The federal government and twenty-nine states do not require work or age permits for youths under 17. Especially in the case of older teenagers, our law provides little legal protection for parental control or input. A teenager in the United States may make long-term education and labor decisions independently, at a time she could not legally buy a bottle of beer or a pack of cigarettes.

Moreover, the FLSA is directed at problems that characterized child labor in the 1930s, not in contemporary America. Most child labor during and prior to the Great Depression resulted from children leaving school to permanently enter the full-time labor force. Only 50 percent of teenagers finished high school then, and nearly a quarter of the United States population lived on farms. Today, a high school diploma is the minimum entry ticket into our current economic society, and agriculture is dominated by large corporations. The modern trend toward part-time rather than full-time adolescent work began in the 1950s and has continued until today when more than 80 percent of high school students report that they have worked during the school year.

"AND OUR FAMILY FRIENDLY POLICY MEANS YOUR CHILDREN CAN WORK HERE TOO."

"And our family friendly policy means your children can work here too," cartoon by Matt Percival. Reproduction rights obtainable from www.CartoonStock.com.

The Concept of Social Neglect

In family law, child neglect is typically defined as "harm or threatened harm to a child's health or welfare . . . by placing a child at unreasonable risk or by failure . . . to intervene to eliminate that risk when that person is able to so do and has, or should have, knowledge of the risk." Such statutes are typically used by state welfare authorities against parents charged with neglect of their child. However, the same concept may be applied to societal neglect of working children in the United States. For more than a century, the Supreme Court has endorsed the pre-existing common-law doctrine of "parens patriae"; i.e., "the supreme power of every state . . . for the prevention of injury to those who cannot protect themselves.". . . Both federal and state governments are guilty of neglect of adolescents who are at risk in the workplace. We have failed in our collective responsibility to these working youth, resulting in death, injury, disease, and blighted futures.

What has produced this scandalous situation? In brief, profits and legal stasis. First, many employers find child workers financially attractive because they provide an immense pool of cheap and easily managed labor. Adolescents almost invariably work for minimum or sub-minimum wage and almost never receive health insurance or other fringe benefits. They accept irregular work schedules, are impossible to organize into trade unions, and can be replaced with minimal retraining or other costs. In addition, adolescents are an enormous market for sellers of goods and services. In 2004, projected adolescent spending totaled $169 billion with fashion items, electronics, restaurants, and entertainment capturing most of this money.

These powerful economic factors are undergirded by legal paralysis. Federal and state laws governing this labor market have not been substantially revised in generations despite enormous increases in the number of children employed and changes in the jobs they perform. There is no organized political force advocating reform. Americans simply do not recognize the problems associated with contemporary child labor. We see this teenage workforce in our daily lives and consume the products and services they create, but we do not "see" the issue. American child labor is a mighty river flowing downhill without obstacle.

> *"[Lowering the minimum wage] would spur employers to hire unskilled workers, creating hundreds of thousands of jobs without costing taxpayers a dime."*

Lowering the Minimum Wage Would Increase Teen Employment

James Sherk

In the following viewpoint, James Sherk contends that young workers in the United States are hobbled by federal mandates that increase the minimum wage. According to Sherk, setting a high minimum wage makes young, unskilled labor less attractive to businesses, effectively keeping young people out of the labor market and depriving them of acquiring skills that could lead to better jobs in the future. Sherk believes if the minimum wage were lowered significantly, more businesses would hire unskilled labor and the unemployment rate for young workers would decrease. Sherk is a senior policy analyst at The Heritage Foundation, a conservative public policy research institution.

The current recession has harmed Americans in almost all walks of life. It has particularly hit America's youth, for whom joblessness has increased far more than for the population as a whole. This has serious long-term consequences for today's youth future employment and earnings and will affect many of them throughout their working lives.

Unfortunately, there are no simple policy solutions to this problem. Congress has spent billions on . . . job-training programs for youth. Evaluations of these programs consistently find that they accomplish little. Evaluations of European youth employment programs have come to the same pessimistic conclusion. Congress should be realistic about the utility of youth employment programs as a policy response.

The best way to improve the job market for youth is to improve the job market overall. The job prospects of less skilled workers improve substantially when labor demand improves. Measures to promote entrepreneurship, business investment, and overall job creation are the best ways to help America's youth find work.

One policy that would specifically improve youth employment would be lowering the minimum wage. The recent minimum wage increase has priced many unskilled teens out of the labor market—depriving them of the opportunity to gain important on-the-job training that would make them more valuable employees. Temporarily reducing the minimum wage to $5.15 an hour would spur hiring of unskilled youth.

The consequences of this recession for youth today pale in comparison to what they will face in the future. The taxes necessary to pay the debts accumulated today will impose a crippling burden on future workers. Today's youth face the prospect of becoming a debt-paying generation who spend their working lives paying off the debt incurred by their parents and grandparents—truly a lost generation.

Difficult Youth Job Prospects

Unemployment has risen across all demographic groups in the recession, and especially for youth. In December 2007 the seasonally adjusted unemployment rate for workers between the ages of 16 and 24 stood at 11.8 percent. By April 2010 it had risen 7.8 percentage points to 19.6 percent: roughly 60 percent greater than the increase in overall unemployment. The figures are worse for teenagers: 25.4 percent of teenagers who want jobs cannot find them.

Disproportionately high youth joblessness is not surprising in a recession. Youth unemployment usually rises more than overall unemployment during economic downturns.

Recessions hit younger workers harder because they have relatively few skills and less experience, making them less productive employees. Employers looking to cut back on their workforces target lower-skilled workers first, both because they contribute less to the enterprises' success and because they are easier to replace when the economy picks up.

New entrants to the labor force face an added difficulty: hiring has dropped sharply in this recession. Many businesses responded to the economic uncertainty by freezing planned expansions. Layoffs also rose substantially as companies struggled to stay afloat but they have now returned to pre-recessionary levels. Hiring has not: This disproportionately hurts young workers looking for work after finishing their education—there are fewer new jobs for them to find.

Long-Term Consequences

High youth unemployment has serious long-term consequences. Workers who start their careers during a recession have less bargaining power to ask for higher wages. Studies show that such wage differences persist throughout their careers.

Workers who begin their careers in a recession are also more likely to wind up in jobs they are less suited for; they take the best job they can find. Unfortunately this permanently affects their careers. A study of college graduates before, during, and after the 1981–82 recession—the last recession as deep as the current downturn—found that workers who graduated in the recession

Some analysts argue that temporarily reducing the minimum wage during economic downturns would make unskilled teens more attractive to employers. © Peter Dazeley/Photographer's Choice/Getty Images.

had lower earnings 15 years later and were less likely to work in desirable occupations.

Other studies point to the same conclusion. Higher minimum wages disproportionately reduce teenage employment. An examination of teenagers in states that raised their minimum wages above the federal rate found they earned lower wages and held fewer jobs up to a decade later. Youth pay a lasting price for forgone experience.

The long-term effects of recessions on youth are not entirely negative. Poor employment prospects spur some students to go to college who would not have otherwise done so. Each percentage point increase in the unemployment rate increases the youth probability of completing college by approximately one percent.

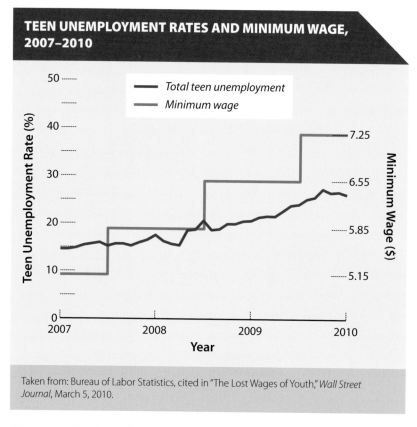

TEEN UNEMPLOYMENT RATES AND MINIMUM WAGE, 2007–2010

Taken from: Bureau of Labor Statistics, cited in "The Lost Wages of Youth," *Wall Street Journal*, March 5, 2010.

However the benefits of this additional schooling do not outweigh the costs on future employment prospects.

Youth Employment Programs Are Ineffective

Congress should resist the urge to respond to the recession by expanding youth employment or training programs. These programs are well intentioned. Unfortunately evaluations show that they accomplish little.

Evaluation studies that randomly assign some workers to "treatment" groups that receive job training or employment subsidies and put other workers in "control" groups . . . do not provide the strongest statistical evidence on whether programs work or not. Program evaluations show that such measures sometimes raise adult earnings and help adult workers find jobs. However, program evaluations almost universally conclude that U.S. youth employment programs accomplish little. . . .

Reduce the Minimum Wage to Spur Youth Employment

Congress has one straightforward and effective policy measure it can take to specifically target youth employment. Congress could suspend the recent minimum wage increase [of July 2009].

Businesses do not hire workers whose labor produces less than the cost of hiring them. Most economic studies unsurprisingly find that increasing the minimum wage reduces employment among low-skilled workers—it prices them out of work. Although individual studies give different estimates, the typical results suggest that in normal economic times a 10 percent increase in the minimum wage reduces employment among heavily affected groups of workers by roughly 2 percent.

The minimum wage disproportionately harms youth employment because many younger workers lack the productivity to command higher wages. About half of minimum wage workers are between the ages of 16 and 24.

Businesses are especially sensitive to higher costs now; few businesses have the profits to pay higher wages out of. So they have responded to this minimum wage hike by reducing their overall payroll costs as much as possible. That has meant hundreds of thousands of fewer jobs for youth and has contributed to the overall increase in youth unemployment.

Putting these youth out of work causes lasting pain because the main value of a minimum wage job is as on-the-job training, not the low wage it pays. Few workers start at the minimum wage and stay there for decades. Rather, most workers take minimum-wage jobs as entry-level positions. Minimum-wage jobs teach unskilled youth valuable job skills, such as how to interact with customers and co-workers or accept direction from a boss. Once workers have gained these skills, they become more productive and earn higher wages. Two-thirds of minimum wage workers earn a raise within a year.

The minimum wage increase from $5.15 to $7.25 an hour has sawed off the bottom rung of many unskilled workers career ladders—higher minimum wages measurably hurt workers' job prospects up to a decade later.

Congress could put these youth back to work by returning the minimum wage to $5.15 an hour until youth unemployment falls below 12 percent. This would spur employers to hire unskilled workers, creating hundreds of thousands of jobs without costing taxpayers a dime. It would provide youth with valuable on-the-job training and experience that will help them earn raises in the future.

Temporarily reducing the minimum wage would mean less pay for some minimum wage workers. However, relatively few of these workers rely on minimum wage jobs to support themselves—almost two-thirds of minimum wage workers work part-time. The benefits of jobs and job training for hundreds of thousands of young workers outweigh these costs.

> "The impact of a minimum wage raise
> on jobs, whether positive or negative,
> is small."

Increasing the Minimum Wage Would Not Increase Teen Unemployment

Heidi Shierholz

In the viewpoint that follows, Heidi Shierholz refutes claims that increasing the minimum wage will lead to higher unemployment among teenagers. She counters that recent drops in teenage employment are a byproduct of recessionary times, not wage hikes. Using government labor statistics, Shierholz argues that fluctuations in the minimum wage have little impact on employment figures. She maintains that all unskilled labor suffers when the economy is bad; however, raising the minimum wage actually puts more spending money in the hands of consumers, thus helping the economy recover. Shierholz is an economist working at the Economic Policy Institute, a nonprofit think tank that addresses economic policy issues.

O n July 24 [2009], in the third and final step of a minimum wage increase enacted by Congress in 2007, the federal minimum wage increased from $6.55 to $7.25, and an estimated 4.5 million of this country's lowest paid workers got a much-needed raise. Over three-quarters—3.4 million—of the affected workers were adults age 20 or older. The other 1.1 million workers were teenagers, age 16–19. Despite the relatively small number of affected teens, this nevertheless represents a large share, 19.9%, of all teen workers. (By comparison, only 2.7% of all workers age 20 and over were affected by the increase.)

Since the minimum wage was raised in July, the teen employment rate (the share of people age 16–19 who are employed) fell from 28.9% to 26.2%. Could this drop plausibly be attributed to July's 70 cent increase in the minimum wage? A careful examination of the data finds no evidence to support that conclusion.

The Recession, Not the Minimum Wage, Is Responsible for Drop in Teen Employment

First, the labor market is in a severe downturn that is affecting essentially all groups. Since the recession started in December 2007, the overall employment rate has fallen from 62.7% to 58.5%, including a decline of 0.9 percentage points since July alone. Figure A shows the overall employment rate, along with the teen employment rate. Both the overall rate and the teen rate have experienced steep declines during the current downturn. The teen rate, however, has fallen farther, as the plot shows is always the case in recessions (recessions are shaded). Teen workers occupy the "last hired, first fired" rung on the job ladder, and their employment is hit much harder during downturns than that of older workers.

Figure B illustrates this further—it shows teen employment as a percent of total employment over time. Because teens are hit harder by downturns than older workers, their share of total employment drops during recessions (and, for the recessions of 1990

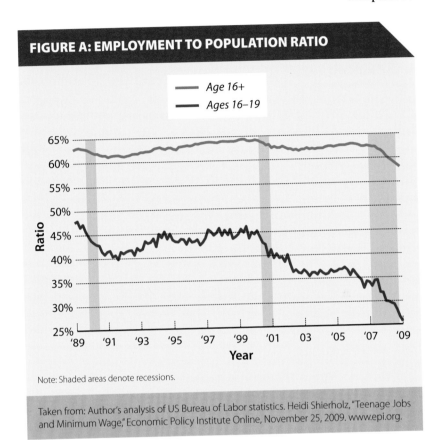

FIGURE A: EMPLOYMENT TO POPULATION RATIO

Age 16+
Ages 16–19

Note: Shaded areas denote recessions.

Taken from: Author's analysis of US Bureau of Labor statistics. Heidi Shierholz, "Teenage Jobs and Minimum Wage," Economic Policy Institute Online, November 25, 2009. www.epi.org.

and 2001, during the period of joblessness that followed them). A quick examination of the plot reveals that far from being an aberration, the decline in the teen share of employment over the last two years is right in line with what would be expected given the length and severity of the current downturn in the labor market.

Instead, Figure B illustrates how teen employment is driven far more by larger labor market employment trends than by any effects of minimum wage changes. The black lines in Figure B mark times when Congress increased the minimum wage to keep up with inflation. The two-step increase in 1990 and 1991 occurred during a period of deterioration in the labor market, and the teen employment share dropped. The two-step increase

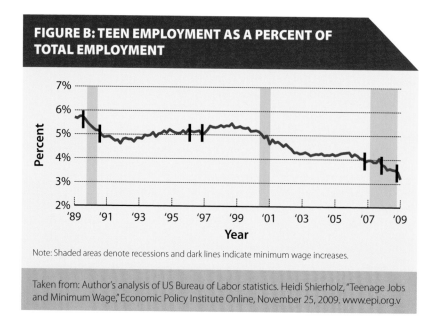

FIGURE B: TEEN EMPLOYMENT AS A PERCENT OF TOTAL EMPLOYMENT

Note: Shaded areas denote recessions and dark lines indicate minimum wage increases.

Taken from: Author's analysis of US Bureau of Labor statistics. Heidi Shierholz, "Teenage Jobs and Minimum Wage," Economic Policy Institute Online, November 25, 2009. www.epi.org.v

in 1996 and 1997 occurred during a strong labor market, and the teen employment share increased. The three-step increase in 2007, 2008, and 2009 occurred during a weak labor market, and the teen employment share fell.

Impact of Minimum Wage Adjustments Is Small

This observation is consistent with what careful empirical studies have found. While it is true that there is some disagreement among economists about whether increasing the minimum wage increases or decreases employment, there is a consensus on the essential point: the impact of a minimum wage raise on jobs, whether positive or negative, is small. The warnings of massive teen job loss due to minimum wage increases simply do not comport with the evidence.

What's more, increasing the minimum wage benefits the economy. An analysis by the Economic Policy Institute, based on research by economists at the Federal Reserve Board of Chicago,

Some analysts believe that the overall state of the economy, not minimum wage changes, make the most impact on teen employment. © Michael L. Abramson/Time & Life Pictures/Getty Images.

found that July's minimum wage increase would contribute $5.5 billion in spending over the 12 months following the increase, by getting additional income into the hands of workers who are likely to be struggling to make ends meet and therefore very likely to spend it. July's minimum wage is providing excellent stimulus for the economy precisely when it needs it the most.

The disastrous economic events of the last two years underscore the need to restore a foundation for the U.S. economy where wages can again grow in tandem with productivity and workers are able to increase their living standards through increased earnings rather than through increased debt. July's increase in the minimum wage, though far short in real terms of restoring the minimum wage to its high-water mark of the late 1960s, was nevertheless an important step in that direction.

| "A lot of jobs are very hard to get. And despite all the bad luck I seemed to have, I didn't give up."

The Struggle to Find a First Job

Personal Narrative

Danielle Wilson

In the following viewpoint, Danielle Wilson, a teenager in New York City, describes her first attempts at securing a summer job. She writes that her inexperience and lack of interview skills led to several disappointments, but she did not quit. After being rejected from some clothing stores and fast food restaurants, she applied for a community-based job to help clean up her neighborhood. Wilson maintains that it may not be the perfect first job, but she realizes many teens have to start at the bottom to work their way up.

A while ago, all of my friends had jobs and I didn't. That's because they had a "hook up." (In case you don't know, a "hook up" is when a person who has a job gets you one with no problem.)

At times, I wished I had a hook up! If I did, I wouldn't have had to go through all those nervous interviews, or waste my ink on those applications that probably got thrown in the trash. If I had a dollar for every time I filled out an application, I wouldn't need a job!

No Experience, No Interview Skills

My job search really started when I turned 16. I went from store to store and filled out applications back to back. One day I asked my grandmother, "Why does no one want to hire me?" She said it was because I didn't have any experience.

How was I supposed to have experience when I'd never had a job before? McDonald's wouldn't even hire me. I applied there so many times it was a shame.

The Gap was one of the hardest places to apply. Once you fill out an application, the managers interview you right on the spot. It made me so nervous that I couldn't talk right.

The first question they ask is, "Why do you want to work for the Gap?" Your mind is telling you to say: "For the money, dummy." But you don't want to say that because you don't want to make yourself sound greedy, even if it's the truth.

So I'd say, "Because I'm familiar with what the company does. Which is sell clothes." (Doesn't the interview sound good so far?)

Yes, but not for long because there was this one question that always seemed to get me every time: "What can you bring to this company?" I don't know, maybe more customers?

Every time they asked me that question, my heart would stop and drop all the way to the floor. By the time I got ready to pick it up, I heard them say, "If we don't contact you in 24 hours, you didn't get the job." I don't know about any of you, but to me that question is hard to answer. I got the impression that the manager wanted me to say a certain thing.

Like, there's one right answer and if I get it wrong, I've failed. But if I was asked that question now, I would say, "I'm a hard worker and a very reliable person, and with those kinds of

EMPLOYED PERSONS 16 TO 24 YEARS OF AGE BY INDUSTRY AND CLASS OF WORKER

Industry and Class of Worker	Total (in thousands)	
	2010	2011
Total employed	18,564	18,632
Agriculture and related industries	372	382
Non-agriculture industries	18,192	18,251
Private wage and salary workers	16,311	16,472
Mining, quarrying, and oil and gas extraction	63	76
Construction	819	744
Manufacturing	1,015	1,106
Durable goods	598	688
Nondurable goods	417	418
Wholesale trade	297	342
Retail trade	3,659	3,869
Transportation and utilities	355	360
Information	361	329
Financial activities	794	716
Professional and business services	1,395	1,326
Education and health services	2,169	1,936
Leisure and hospitality	4,595	4,770
Other services	789	898
Government wage and salary workers	1,433	1,382
Federal	221	190
State	443	452
Local	769	739
Self-employed and unpaid family workers	447	397

Taken from: US Bureau of Labor Statistics, August 24, 2011.

abilities I cannot only do a good job, but I can influence other employees to do so too."

Any Age Problem

One time I was so close to getting a job at Burger King. My friend Cindy, who was supposed to be my "hook up," told her manager that she had a friend who wanted to work there. So I went down, filled out an application, and handed it to the manager personally. He called me two days later and told me to come down the next day and bring my working papers, Social Security card and a picture ID.

I was so excited when he called, I started jumping up and down screaming, "Grandma, I got the job, I got the job!" Like I won the lottery or something.

The next day I went down there early for my interview. The manager was in a meeting, so he sent the assistant manager to interview me. (Mind you, she was new.)

During the interview the assistant manager was asking me simple stuff that I could answer on the drop of a dime. Then she asked, "How old are you?"

"Sixteen, miss."

"Oh, I'm sorry, you have to be 16 and a half to work here." I exploded. "Why do you have to be 16 and a half?" I said in a not-so-nice tone.

She said, "Because you have to work with a grill and hot oil." "But what does being 16 and a half got to do with it?"

"Because . . ." she tried to say. "I don't want to hear it, miss. That doesn't make any sense. Can I please speak to the manager?" I yelled. "You'll have to wait until he gets out of the meeting."

"Then I'll wait," I said.

So I waited a half an hour, watching the assistant manager interview other people, including my other friend Shantel. She got the job with no problems, because she was 17.

When the manager came out I immediately went toward him and asked, "How old do you have to be to work here?"

"Sixteen," he said.

"Why did the assistant manager tell me that I have to be 16 and a half?"

"I didn't tell her that," the assistant manager said. "I put a question mark on her application because she attends school in the day and you told me you were taking people that could work during the day."

"Oh, you're right," the manager said. And he walked out of the store before I could tell him that my friend got hired and goes to school. I looked at the lady and rolled my eyes.

But after I thought about it, I realized that I shouldn't have yelled and acted like I did. That was very unprofessional. I should have just left it alone, said, "Thank you," and walked away.

Going into a Group Interview

During the holidays, I tried Gap again. I answered all the manager's questions. My heart was going to drop, but I held onto it.

After the interview I got kind of excited because the manager said, "OK," took out a piece of paper, handed it to me and said, "You have a group interview on the 2nd of December at 4:30. Be there a half-hour early." My heart made a complete stop.

A group interview is when you're not the only one getting interviewed. The manager interviews several people at the same time. I was kind of disappointed because I thought I was going to be hired on the spot. But another part of me was excited because I had never gotten this far with the Gap before.

On the day of the group interview I got there an hour early. I know, I was desperate, but it's good to get there early.

By the time 4:30 came, there were eight girls including myself. Well, to me the interview was fun. The manager gave each of us a card and we had to pretend that we worked there and were picking out an outfit for the person described on the card.

My person was a female looking for an outfit to wear for a date. She didn't want anything loose or baggy, and she didn't want anything in denim.

So I picked out a black skirt and a black dressy shirt and a little handbag. During the interview we had to describe the outfits we picked and why. Then the manager asked us some questions and the interview was over. She told us that if we didn't get called for a third interview, then try again next year.

Third interview?! What do they think, working at the Gap is a career? I didn't get called.

But I learned, through McDonald's and the Gap, that a lot of jobs are very hard to get. And despite all the bad luck I seemed to have, I didn't give up. Eventually, I finally found a summer job.

Starting at the Bottom

There was a summer job program in New York City that I never knew about while I was applying at fast food restaurants. If you live in a housing project like myself, you may qualify. You have to do almost everything, like keeping the projects clean. (I don't mind being in the sun; I need a tan.)

I know some of you are thinking, "I'm not cleaning up for nobody." I was thinking the same way. But hey, it paid minimum wage and it was a job. And cleaning isn't that bad!

Besides, you have to start at the bottom before you reach the top. And the next time I looked for a job, it was that much easier. I already had work experience.

> "The government has failed to address the unequal treatment of working children in the Fair Labor Standards Act (FLSA), which provides fewer protections to children working in agriculture."

Child Farm Workers Should Be Held to the Same Regulations as Other Young Workers

Human Rights Watch

In the following viewpoint, Human Rights Watch reports that it is unfair that child farm laborers are exempt from some of the strict regulations that apply to young workers in non-farm employment. The organization states that children can labor on farms at very young ages and undertake hazardous work that would be prohibited in non-farm occupations. In addition, Human Rights Watch maintains that young people are often employed for longer hours with less pay than their counterparts in non-farm jobs. This is especially a concern for the numerous illegal immigrant child laborers who, along with their families, fear deportation if they balk at wages or working conditions. Human Rights Watch believes that the government should change the laws so that child farm workers are afforded the same protections as other child laborers and that existing safeguards should be fully enforced to ensure the fair treatment of all young workers. Human Rights Watch is an international watchdog agency that monitors civil rights abuses, including the exploitation of child labor.

Hundreds of thousands of children under age 18 are working in agriculture in the United States. But under a double standard in US federal law, children can toil in the fields at far younger ages, for far longer hours, and under far more hazardous conditions than all other working children. For too many of these children, farmwork means an early end to childhood, long hours at exploitative wages, and risk to their health and sometimes their lives. Although their families' financial need helps push children into the fields—poverty among farmworkers is more than double that of all wage and salary employees—the long hours and demands of farmwork result in high drop-out rates from school. Without a diploma, child workers are left with few options besides a lifetime of farmwork and the poverty that accompanies it.

In 2000, Human Rights Watch published the report "Fingers to the Bone: United States Failure to Protect Child Farmworkers." This study documented the exploitative, dangerous conditions under which children worked in agriculture and the damage inflicted upon their health and education. Highlighting weak protections in US law, it found that even these provisions were rarely enforced. Nearly 10 years later, Human Rights Watch returned to the fields to assess conditions for working children. We conducted research in the states of Florida, Michigan, North Carolina and Texas, interviewing dozens of child farmworkers who had altogether worked in 14 states across the country. Shockingly, we found that conditions for child farmworkers in the United States remain virtually as they were a decade ago. This report details those conditions and the failure of the US government to take effective steps needed to remedy them. Most notably, the government has failed to address the unequal treatment of working

Youth labor advocates argue that child farm workers are not adequately protected by US federal law. Child agriculture workers often work in more hazardous conditions and for longer hours than in other occupations. © Lowell Georgia/National Geographic/Getty Images.

children in the Fair Labor Standards Act (FLSA), which provides fewer protections to children working in agriculture compared with all other working children.

In agriculture, children typically start working adult hours during the summers, weekends, or after school at age 11 or 12. Many children work part time much earlier, and Human Rights Watch interviewed child farmworkers as young as seven. Seventeen-year-old Jose M., who described the shock he felt going to work at age 11, said that when he looks around the field and sees 12-year-olds, "I know how they feel. I used to feel like that. They have a face that says they don't want to be here." He added, "Teachers at school know when kids turn 12. They see the cuts on their hands. They know a child at 12 goes to work. No if's, and's, or but's."

Parents told us they took their children to work because they did not have childcare and because they needed the money to meet basic expenses and buy school supplies. The fact that the work is legal also presents it as a legitimate choice for parents, children, and employers. But several mothers later expressed regret over the choices they had made. One mother in Texas said she believed she had already stolen her 11-year-old daughter's childhood. Another said when she saw what work did to her two oldest children, she decided not to take her two youngest children to work.

Farm Work Conditions for Children

Current US law provides no minimum age for children working on small farms so long as they have their parents' permission. Children ages 12 and up may work for hire on any farm with their parents' consent, or if they work with their parents on the same farm. Once children reach age 14, they can work on any farm even without their parents' permission. Outside of agriculture, children must be at least 16 years old to work, with a few exceptions: 14- and 15-year-olds can work in specified jobs such as cashiers, grocery baggers, and car washers, subject to very restricted conditions.

Children often work 10 or more hours a day: at the peak of the harvest they may work daylight to dusk, with few breaks. Children described working five to seven days a week, weather permitting. For example, 14-year-old Olivia A. said she worked from 6 A.M. to 6 or 7 P.M. picking blueberries in Michigan, seven days a week. Felix D., age 15, said he worked the same hours deflowering tobacco in North Carolina, six days a week.

For school children, work is often confined to weekends and summers, and before and after school. Children who have dropped out of school, including "unaccompanied children" who have come without their families from Mexico and Central America, work these hours whenever work is available. Under US law, there are no limits on the hours children can work in agriculture outside of school hours. In non-agricultural settings, 14- and 15-year-olds cannot work more than three hours on a school day and eight hours on a non-school day.

Children working in agriculture typically make less than the minimum wage. Their pay is often further cut because employers underreport hours, and they are forced to spend their own money on tools, gloves, and drinking water that their employers should provide by law. For example, in the Texas panhandle region, children told us they made $45 to $50 a day for 10 or more hours of hoeing cotton, or at best $4.50 to $5.00 an hour, compared with the federal hourly minimum wage of $7.25. Where the pay is based on a piece rate, meaning workers are paid by the quantity they pick, it is usually much worse. Antonio M., age 12, said that picking blueberries on piece rate in North Carolina, he made at most $3.60 an hour.

With some notable exceptions, farmworkers are legally entitled to minimum wage but not overtime, and rarely receive job-related benefits that much of the rest of America's workforce takes for granted. They receive no paid sick days, no health insurance, no paid vacation leave, and have no job security. They only get paid for the hours they work. Laws that deny farmworkers overtime, and in some instances minimum wage, combined with poor enforcement of existing wage laws, contribute to farmworkers' poverty and financial desperation that compel children to work and make farmworkers even more vulnerable to exploitation. . . .

Low Standards on Hazardous Work

Agriculture is the most dangerous industry for young workers, according to the Centers for Disease Control's National Institute for Occupational Safety and Health (NIOSH). Working with sharp tools and heavy machinery, exposed to chemicals, climbing up tall ladders, lugging heavy buckets and sacks, children get hurt and sometimes they die. From 2005 to 2008, at least 43 children under age 18 died from work-related injuries in crop production—27 percent of all children who were fatally injured at work. The risk of fatal injuries for agricultural workers ages 15 to 17 is more than 4 times that of other young workers.

Under current US law, children can do agricultural work that the US Department of Labor deems "particularly hazardous" for children at age 16 (and at any age on farms owned or operated by their parents). In non-agricultural sectors, no one under age 18 can do such jobs. Incongruously, some of the same jobs that are considered too dangerous for teenagers in non-agricultural settings are perfectly legal in agriculture: a 16-year-old who is barred from driving a forklift in a store warehouse, for example, may do so without restriction on a farm.

Children routinely described small injuries, and some more serious in interviews with Human Rights Watch. Rarely did they say they sought medical care. Jose M. said he was 12 when "they gave me my first knife. Week after week I was cutting myself. Every week I had a new scar. My hands have a lot of stories. There are scars all over." Another boy described being hurt when the truck carrying him out to the field rear-ended another. Nevertheless, he said, he and his family returned to work the next day: working sick, injured, and without taking breaks was a common theme among our interviewees who needed the money and were afraid of getting fired if they missed a day.

Human Rights Watch saw children working without gloves and even barefoot. Most said no one required them to wear protective gear; if anyone, it was their parents who urged them to wear it, not their employers.

Children often work performing the same motions—kneeling, stooping, or raising their arms for hours a day. Youth described pain in their backs, knees, hands, and feet, even at very young ages. Children whose bodies are still developing are especially vulnerable to repetitive-motion injury.

Children work in extreme temperatures, heat and cold, from over 110 degrees in the Texas summer to snow in Michigan. In some climates the day starts cold and wet, then turns unbearably hot. Elias N., age 16, said the bad days for him were the "real hot ones, the field is full of weeds, you can't even take a step. When you're surrounded by corn, there's no air." Working long hours in high temperatures places children at risk of heat stroke and dehydration, particularly if there is not enough drinking water. Heat illnesses can lead to brain damage and death, and children are significantly more susceptible to heat stress than adults. A 17-year-old girl in California died in May 2008 after working nine hours pruning grape vines. Her supervisor delayed her seeking medical care, and when she finally reached the hospital she had a core body temperature of 108 degrees.

Employers Often Provide Few or No Amenities

Many children said that their employers did not provide drinking water, handwashing facilities, or toilets. Children described bringing their own water and sometimes running out. In some places workers said they had to buy water with their meager wages because the quality of the water in migrant housing was too poor to drink. The federal Occupational Safety and Health Administration (OSHA) requires agricultural employers to provide drinking water, water for hand washing, and toilet facilities. Congress, however, exempts farms with fewer than 11 employees from these regulations, essentially exempting them from having to protect their workers' dignity and most basic health requirements.

The Dangers of Pesticide Exposure

Children are exposed to pesticides. Some children told Human Rights Watch they were sprayed directly; many more said that the fields next to them were sprayed while they were working, and they smelled and had reactions to the drift. "Here there are a lot of chemicals in the field," said 18-year-old Hector H., who worked alongside children. "You can smell them. [Recently] the plane sprayed, sprayed the cotton. . . . I felt dizzy. I covered my face and kept working. No one told us to get out of the field." Many children described seeing residue on the plants or even going back into fields wet with spray. Almost none of the children we spoke with had received training on pesticide safety.

Exposure to pesticides is a hazard for all farmworkers but may be especially dangerous for children whose bodies are still developing. Children are uniquely vulnerable to chemicals and may absorb pesticides more easily than adults. Children working in agriculture have far greater incidence rates of acute occupational pesticide-related illnesses than children working in other jobs. Exposures to pesticides can produce rash, dizziness, nausea and vomiting, headaches, and burning eyes, as well as brain damage and death. Long-term pesticide exposure in adults is associated with chronic health problems such as cancer, neurologic problems, and reproductive problems.

US Environmental Protection Agency (EPA) regulations prohibit the spraying of pesticides when any unprotected worker is in the field or may be exposed through drift. The agency sets restricted-entry intervals (REIs) specifying the amount of time after pesticide application workers should not be in treated areas and requires basic pesticide safety training for all workers. However, EPA regulations make no special consideration for children. They do not prohibit children mixing, handling, or

FEDERAL AND STATE LAWS THAT RESTRICT AGE OF CHILD AGRICULTURAL EMPLOYMENT

State	Minimum Age for Employment	
	During School Hours	Outside School Hours
Federal: Fair Labor Standards Act (FLSA) applies to migrants and local residents regardless of farm size or number of man-days of farm labor used on that farm.	16	14, 12 with written parental consent or on farm where parent is employed. Under 12 with written parental consent on farms exempt from minimum wage provisions
Alaska	16	14
Arizona	16	14
Arkansas	16	14
California	18, 16 if not required to attend school	12
Colorado	16	12
Connecticut (separate agriculture child labor law)	16	14
Delaware (farm work exempt unless performed in hazardous occupations)	----	----
Florida	----	14
Hawaii	18, 16 if not legally required to attend school	14, 15 in pineapple harvesting, 10 in coffee harvesting
Idaho	16	----

FEDERAL AND STATE LAWS THAT RESTRICT AGE OF CHILD AGRICULTURAL EMPLOYMENT (continued)

State	Minimum Age for Employment	
	During School Hours	Outside School Hours
Illinois (minimum age only)	12	10
Indiana (exempt except for minimum age or when school is in session)	---	12
Iowa Law exempts part-time work in agriculture (less that 20 hours a week when school is not in session and less than 14 hours a week while school is in session). It covers all migratory labor. Law exempts work in the production of seed, limited to removal of off-type plants, corn tassels and hand-pollinating during June, July and August for children 14 and over.	16	14, 12 migratory labor (younger with permit from Labor Commissioner upon court order)
Maine (exempt if not in direct contact with hazardous machinery or substances)	16, unless excused by superintendant of schools	--- except 14 if in direct contact with hazardous machinery or substances
Massachusetts	16	---
Michigan (exempt except for operations involving detasseling, roguing, hoeing, or similar in production of seed)	16	13

FEDERAL AND STATE LAWS THAT RESTRICT AGE OF CHILD AGRICULTURAL EMPLOYMENT (continued)

State	Minimum Age for Employment	
	During School Hours	Outside School Hours
Minnesota	16	12
Missouri	16	14
Nevada (exempt except for minimum age when school is in session)	14	----
New Hampshire	18, 16 if not enrolled in school	12
New Jersey	16	12
New Mexico	16, 14 in hardship cases	----
New York	16	14, 12 hand harvest berries, fruits and vegetables
North Dakota	14	----
Ohio	16	14
Oregon	16	12, 9 picking berries or beans for intrastate use with parental permission
Pennsylvania (exempt from child labor law. Separate law covers seasonal farm workers.)	----	---- seasonal farm worker under 14 not to be required to work
South Carolina	16	14, 12 with parental approval

	Minimum Age for Employment	
State	**During School Hours**	**Outside School Hours**
South Dakota	---	---
Utah	16	12, no limit with parental consent
Vermont	16, 14 with certification	---
Virginia	16	14, 12 with parental consent
Washington	18	14, 12 hand-harvesting or cultivating berries, bulbs, cucumbers and spinach during non-school week
Wisconsin	18	12

FEDERAL AND STATE LAWS THAT RESTRICT AGE OF CHILD AGRICULTURAL EMPLOYMENT (continued)

Taken from: US Department of Labor, Wage and Hour Division, "State Child Labor Laws Applicable to Agricultural Employment," January 1, 2011. www.dol.gov.

applying pesticides (although regulations on hazardous work prohibit children under age 16 from using the most dangerous categories of pesticides). Pesticide risk assessments do not take children's special vulnerabilities into account. REIs are set using a 154-pound adult male as a model—they are not adapted for children, pregnant women, or others who differ from this model. . . .

Regulatory Agencies Lag in Enforcement of Child Protection Laws

Despite these risks to children's health and safety, even the weak protections in US law are rarely enforced. Indeed, in the 10 years following the publication of our first report, enforcement of child labor laws overall by the Department of Labor's Wage and Hour division declined dramatically. In 2009 the division found only 36 cases of child labor violations in agriculture, constituting only 4 percent of all child labor violations, compared with 104 cases in 1998. In 2008 Congress raised the maximum civil money penalties for violations of child labor provisions resulting in death or serious injury, and in 2009 the Department of Labor added several hundred new labor inspectors and promised more robust enforcement of labor laws. It remained to be seen at the time of writing whether these efforts would result in better protection for child farmworkers.

Although each has recently undertaken positive steps in this direction, neither the US Department of Labor nor the EPA has made regulatory changes to better protect child farmworkers from dangerous work and pesticides. Many of the regulations specifying "particularly hazardous" jobs are out of date and fail to address the serious safety and health hazards that children face in the workplace. In 2002 NIOSH recommended in a lengthy report that the Department of Labor update many of the so-called "hazardous order" regulations. By early 2010, the department had taken steps towards updating some of the regulations for non-agricultural jobs but had not placed amending the list for agriculture on its published regulatory agenda, despite the particularly dangerous nature of agricultural labor and younger age at which children are permitted to do hazardous jobs. Nor has the Wage and Hour Division enforced existing prohibitions on hazardous work: in 2009 it cited only two violations of agricultural hazardous orders in two cases, or 0.14 percent of the 1,432 hazardous order violations it found that year.

In December 2009, the EPA announced plans to strengthen its assessment of pesticide health risks for children, farmworkers and others, with a strong emphasis on risks for children in the fields. A process to amend the Worker Protection Standard, which regulates practices related to workers' exposure to pesticides, has been ongoing for more than a decade.

Lax enforcement of labor laws and health and safety standards is exacerbated by workers' fears of reporting violations to authorities because they fear deportation for themselves or for their family members. While many child farmworkers are US citizens, the entire family may fear deportation if the parents are undocumented or hold short-term agricultural visas.

Labor standards and their enforcement apply to all workers, irrespective of their immigration status. However, enforcement of workplace protection laws often relies upon workers to self-report abuse. They are very unlikely to do so when their employers can threaten to call the US Immigration and Customs Enforcement agency (ICE). Workers are also unlikely to report abuses to local police or law enforcement, since these agencies are increasingly involved in enforcing immigration laws.

The United States Is Violating International Law

The United States spent over $26 million in 2009 to eliminate child labor around the world—more than all other countries combined—yet the country's law and practice concerning child farmworkers are in violation of or are inconsistent with international conventions on the rights of children. International Labor Organization Convention No. 182 on the Worst Forms of Child Labor, ratified by the United States in 1999, prohibits children from engaging in dangerous or harmful work. The Convention on the Rights of the Child, to which the United States is a signatory but not a party, seeks to protect children from economic exploitation, and also from work that is hazardous or otherwise harmful. Additionally, because farmworker children are overwhelmingly ethnically Hispanic, the disparity in legal protections provided to agricultural workers compared to other workers in the United States has a disparate impact that is discriminatory under international law. The failure of the United States to enforce existing laws and regulations that purport to protect children working in agriculture further violate the United States' international legal obligations.

For the last decade, members of Congress have repeatedly introduced draft legislation into both the Senate and House of Representatives that would eliminate the double-standard in US child labor laws, and apply the same age and hour restrictions to children working in agriculture that already apply to other in-dustries. However, none of the bills have ever reached a vote.

> "Thanks to the ... U.S. Department
> of Labor, youngsters who have the
> advantage of growing up and working
> on a farm might as well move in with
> their city cousins."

Child Farm Workers
Should Not Be Subject to
Unreasonable Regulation

Stu Ellis

In the following viewpoint, Stu Ellis argues against new regulations the US Department of Labor is proposing to curtail child labor in agriculture. Ellis contends that young people are needed on family farms, and their work helps ensure that the next generation of farmers will be well-trained. Ellis fears that if the Department of Labor's changes take effect, too many young people will be discouraged from taking over farms and renewing a vital industry in the United States. Ellis is a former farm business and marketing educator with the University of Illinois Extension.

If you are a farm kid, raise your hand. Now, everyone else look at those whose hands are raised because they will soon be as scarce as a World War II veteran. Yes, thanks to the omniscient folks at the U.S. Department of Labor, youngsters who have the

Thirty US Senators Oppose the Department of Labor's Proposed Rule to Restrict Child Labor in Agriculture

We would like to emphasize the Department [of Labor] was under no obligation to propose new regulations. Congress has not amended the Fair Labor Standards Act (FLSA) in regard to the agricultural standards referenced in the proposed rule since 1977. It is puzzling why the Department would suddenly propose changes to existing regulations, particularly considering the advancements in farm equipment and adoption of technologies that have improved operator safety in the last 35 years.

The Department's belief that it should pursue "parity between the agricultural and nonagricultural child labor provisions" is a misguided interpretation of the FLSA. Congress enacted different standards in the FLSA specifically to address the different occupational situations faced in agriculture compared to other areas of employment. The FLSA does not contain, nor has Congress ever approved, the concept of "parity" between agricultural and nonagricultural sectors. The Department should abandon its goal of parity unless specifically authorized to do so in the future by Congress.

Jerry Moran, Ben Nelson, and twenty-eight
other US senators, Letter to Hilda L. Solis,
US Department of Labor Secretary,
December 19, 2011.

advantage of growing up and working on a farm might as well move in with their city cousins.

The newly proposed regulations from the Department of Labor will delay the education of a farm kid well past the point he or she may ever want to return to the farm. Ag restrictions are being placed on what can be done at certain ages.

Sorry, can't go out to the machine shed, you'll be hurt. Sorry, can't go to the barn, you'll be hurt. Sorry, can't mow the lawn, you'll be hurt. Sorry, can't touch the family GPS unit, you'll be hurt. Oh, and don't even think about going near the county fair livestock show ring, Dad or Mom will be showing your 4-H and FFA [Future Farmers of America] projects because you'll be hurt, if you try that.

It is not a thrill to read the 50 pages in the Federal Register where such new regulations are proposed, but it was published September 2, [2011] beginning on page 54836. . . .

Reducing Opportunities for the Next Generation of Farmers

The Department of Labor is proposing new rules for the Child Labor Act. Not many farm kids would consider themselves slaves, because they would rather be with Mom and Dad learning what happens on the farm, with hands-on, on the job training.

However the restrictions being proposed will severely reduce those opportunities, and in some cases eliminate them until they are at least 16, and in some cases 18 years of age.

The Department of Labor does make a distinction between kids working for their parents and kids working for a non-parent. There are fewer restrictions for kids working for their parents than the non-parents, possibly because the regulation writers think parents will keep an eye peeled more often than Granddad to prevent a tragic use of a two-way radio. After all, summoning someone to come in for lunch could be fatal if the two-way radio was not used properly, I guess.

The partial exemptions for farm kids helping at home come to an abrupt halt if the operator is not father or mother. Working on the farm of an uncle, grandfather, older brother or cousin is not acceptable. In those cases, all prohibitions are back on.

But there is another critical prohibition and that occurs if the teenager is paid by the family corporation. Such an entity is not a parent, and regardless of the supervisor, the proposals will not allow it.

These proposals could become part of the Child Labor Act unless changes are made, and the Department of Labor is accepting comments through December 1 [2011].

The Need for Younger Farmers

One of those submitting comments may be Secretary of Agriculture Tom Vilsack because the proposed regulations are very embarrassing for him. No, he doesn't have a 13 year old driving a tractor back on an Iowa farm. But Secretary Vilsack has been speaking out strongly about the need to create farming opportunities for young people.

On January 20 in Washington, Vilsack addressed the National FFA officers and said, "I would like for you to work with your fellow students and the adult leadership of the organization to develop a series of recommendations around the upcoming Farm Bill that will encourage more young people to pursue careers in farming. Over the next few years we will need 100,000 new farmers and I am looking to you for ideas, guidance and suggestions to help make that happen. If you do this in a serious thoughtful manner (which I know you will do) I will make myself and all of my Under Secretaries available to hear this report. So that we can utilize this information to guide our input to Congress, I would like to have your report to me one year from today."

And on October 24, in Ankeny, IA, Vilsack laid out his Farm Bill priorities, expressing concern about the average age of farmers adding, "The average American farmer is 57 years of age. Nearly 30 percent of American farmers are over the age of 65, which is almost double the number of folks in the workforce over 65. Now, some of these folks want to slow down or retire; but they have no one to take over the farming operation. That challenges us to find new ways, through tax policy, through regulations, through our credit programs or other programs, to help transition farms to the next generation. We'll need a com-

A fourteen-year-old boy feeds pigs on his family's farm in Nebraska. Critics argue that proposed US Department of Labor regulations would prevent children from learning farming practices and deplete the agriculture workforce. © AP Images/Nati Harnik.

munity effort to recruit, train, and support this new generation of farmers and ranchers; and we need to make sure that it's for operations of all sizes."

Mr. Secretary, just like a corn kernel grows into a stalk of corn, a farm kid grows up to be a farmer. You have to start with a seed, and your federal colleagues at the Department of Labor have been plowing up your corn field.

| "*Effort is something that we all learn at a very young age.*"

Learning That Hard Work Leads to a Better Life

Personal Narrative

Melissa Gonzalez

In the following viewpoint, eighteen-year-old Melissa Gonzalez describes her life as a Hispanic migrant worker. Gonzalez writes that her family has always lived the migratory life, following farm work where it was available. She states that she is proud of her labor and the fact that she has always been able to keep up with her school work despite moving around the United States. She attests that, because she is focused and determined, she will fulfill her dreams of going to college and becoming an attorney so she can make a difference in her community.

From [the Mexican cities of] Cuahuila to San Luis Potosi, all the way to Vallermoso to a small town called Caldwell, Texas my roots flow. Being a [migrant] and of Hispanic heritage has been one of the greatest things in my life. Though many Hispanics find being of this race difficult I believe all the opposite. Coming from a family of hard workers and full of effort can only make you want only the best for you and your future.

The Migration Cycle

Effort is something that we all learn at a very young age. I discovered it when I was only 10 years old. We had migrated to Minnesota and it was the first year I entered a field of labor. I learned that without effort food would not be in the tables of many people in the U.S. My family and I have acquired many goals. Though people migrate because of need they play an important role in the cycle of life. My father has migrated all his life. Once my father and mother married both have migrated since marriage till the current year [2004]. They have accumulated quite a list of farm work since they first started migrating. All this farm work on the list ranges from truck driving, planting, irrigating, hoeing to picking, clipping, cutting, canning, detaseling, and stacking.

Keeping up with School Work

Being a migrant was not difficult for me but was a challenge I knew I could conquer. Working together my brothers, sisters and I we would be ready to start school the very next day that we would arrive from up north. We knew that we would be a month behind in our schooling so we worked together to be ready once we arrived. We put our heads together and came up with different ways to not miss another day than we had to. Yes, migrating affected us by the disadvantage of not being able to start school on the very first day, but we were always ready with a spare change of clothes to change that very morning we arrived from the long journey back to our home town. We were up and ready to catch up on what we needed to. Coming late was never an excuse for me. All in my senior year I took advantage of the time and I acquired 12 college hours in English 1301, Music Appreciation, Government, and the Spanish AP exam.

AGE WHEN STARTING FARM WORK (2005–2009)	
Age of Farmworker	**Percent**
12 years or younger	4%
13–17 years	26%
18–20 years	23%
21 years or older	48%

Taken from: National Agricultural Survey 2005–2009, cited in Bon Appétit Management Company Foundation and United Farm Workers, "Inventory of Farmworker Issues and Protections in the United States," March 2011.

Also currently I am taking English 1302, College Algebra, and Economics, which will give me 9 more college credit hours. I have worked very hard and put much effort in these classes to obtain the grade that is needed to receive these hours. Working hard with much to do in my hands I still made time to be in U.I.L. [University Interscholastic League of Texas] Public Speaking, FBLA (Future Business Leaders of America) Public Speaking II, and U.I.L. Current Events. In U.I.L. Public Speaking I have placed in many invitational meets and will be going to district this year and trying my best to get all to way to state. With all my achievements I have earned the National Honor Roll. I have also been recognized as an honors student which I am very proud of. I thank my father for he has been my biggest motivation in life.

Looking Toward the Future

Though we naturally migrate my family did not migrate on the year of 2002, because of my father and I. He helped me conquer my dream of visiting Washington D.C. I not only conquered my dream but toured . . . [the] Capital of the United States for one week. I achieved this by what now makes me think twice of who and what I am, a migrant. [Because] of this trip I received a certificate of completion of the Democracy Leadership Program of Bert Corona. The sight of Washington D.C. motivated me and made me realize that anybody can get a higher education after high school. The major that I am striving for is to become an attorney. As a minority—because I am Hispanic and [a] woman— I am aware that getting into the law field will not be easy. This is why it has become my goal. I can and will become an attorney. It is important to me to make this my future career because one of my life goals to make a difference in my community and for it to spread. As an attorney I will be placing violators of the law behind bars. I believe that everybody should follow the law, for without the world would be chaos. I know that this will not be easy but I know that to conquer a dream it takes hard work and effort.

Being the first graduate from my family has motivated tremendously and I believe that I am ready to take the next step . . . attending a post-secondary school. My dad once told me, "Never be satisfied with what you get; always strive for more." Taking his advice, I will never be satisfied with a bachelor's degree but will go for a doctor degree, and the one and only thing that has motivated me to do this is the fact that I am a migrant.

> *"The ideal solution to prevent the continued exploitation of children in reality programming is for Congress to enact a federal statute that clearly protects them."*

Children in Reality Television Shows Should Be Protected by Labor Laws

Dayna B. Royal

In the following viewpoint, Dayna B. Royal argues that children in reality television programs are insufficiently protected by child labor laws. She maintains children in reality shows are commonly considered free labor despite the fact that they "perform" long hours and have their lives interrupted—even overwhelmed—by work. Royal believes child actor exemptions in current laws are inappropriate for reality performers because the children in reality television are often compelled against their wishes to act. She contends that the US Congress needs to pass a statute to prohibit the use of children of a certain age in reality programming and clearly define when those of eligible age can work. Royal is an assistant law professor in the Cumberland School of Law at Alabama's Samford University.

Dayna B. Royal, "Jon & Kate Plus the State: Why Congress Should Protect Children in Reality Programming," *Akron Law Review*, 2010, pp. 435–500. Copyright © 2010 by Akron Law Review. All rights reserved. Reproduced by permission.

The use of children in reality programming involves employment, which implicates labor laws. Neither the relevant federal labor law—the Fair Labor Standards Act ("FLSA")—nor relevant state laws sufficiently protect children in reality programming. In fact, an exemption in the FLSA prevents it from applying to these children entirely. While state laws vary, the extent of their protection for children in reality programming is generally unclear. And to the extent they do apply to these children, they do not provide enough protection to ensure that these children do not suffer psychological wounds from the sale of their privacy.

Further, state laws are insufficient to protect children in reality programming because program executives may evade them by filming in states with more lenient laws, leaving children in some states more vulnerable than in others. The ideal solution to prevent the continued exploitation of children in reality programming is for Congress to enact a federal statute that clearly protects them.

Reality Programming Is Child Labor

As an introductory matter, it is important to note that when children participate in reality programming, they perform labor properly subject to labor laws. Reality programming employs children (albeit, often through their parents) to provide entertainment. It does so with relatively inexpensive labor costs. It has thus been described [by Jeff Hermanson, assistant executive director of the Writers Guild of America, West] as "'the sweatshop of the entertainment industry.'"

The children engaged to provide such entertainment experience their participation as work. The Gosselin children's [of the show *Jon & Kate Plus 8*] aunt and uncle reported that the children "[we]re very aware of the cameras in their home," and they did not wish to participate in *Jon & Kate*. They often cried because they did not want to be filmed. They were unable to relax in their own home because the show transformed it into a never-ending workplace.

The young cast members of the television show Kid Nation *worked up to fourteen hours a day while being constantly filmed.* © Monty Brinton/CBS Photo Archive/Getty Images.

The *Kid Nation* stars understand this. They worked fourteen-hour days without reprieve while filming. Many of the children said that the most challenging part of the project was being filmed constantly, even during private moments. One child initially thought the project sounded like a fun adventure until he arrived and realized it was "annoying" work. These children understand that reality programming employs children to perform work rather than to participate in life experiences captured on tape.

To legitimate the cheap labor, however, producers maintain the contrary, "rely[ing] on the tradition of documentary to make it seem like it's not exploitation when the only true commitment [producers] have is to turn a profit [according to Mark Andrejevìc, author of *Reality TV: The Work of Being Watched*]." They argue that participants are merely living in front of the cameras and thus, labor laws should not apply.

An associate professor of communication studies at the University of Iowa and author of a book on reality television, Mark Andrejevìc, thinks this is absurd. "'[W]ork means submitting to conditions that are set by employers in order to generate profit for those employers. . . . [T]he only reason you can say that kids [in reality programming] are not working is because they're not getting paid or are underpaid. In any other industry, this would be called exploitation.'"

Indeed, courts have long agreed that "work" occurs despite no compensation or formal employment. Because employment in reality programming is labor, the government should regulate it as such. . . .

The FLSA Does Not Protect These Children

The FLSA governs child labor. Congress enacted the FLSA pursuant to its Commerce Clause power. Though the FLSA governs child labor, it expressly exempts from coverage children employed as "actor[s] or performer[s]."

The Secretary of Labor has defined "performer" broadly to include anyone who:

> performs a distinctive, personalized service as a part of an actual broadcast or telecast including . . . any person who entertains, affords amusement to, or occupies the interest of a radio or television audience by . . . announcing, or describing or relating facts, events and other matters of interest, and who actively participates in such capacity in the actual presentation of a radio or television program.

Though cases have not addressed whether children in reality programming fall within this exemption, from the plain language of the definition, it seems clear that they do. They occupy the interest of their audience by relating facts, events, and other matters as they go about their daily lives. Because children in reality programming are likely "performers" within the meaning of the FLSA, they are exempt from its protection.

This is unsettling. One wonders whether in 1949 the drafters of this exemption ever contemplated that it might one day apply to children forced to live their real lives on camera. It is doubtful that they did given that they did not actually define "performer" in the exemption. That definition instead comes from a 1951 federal regulation, which borrows the definition from another regulation adopted in 1950 that defines "performer" in an entirely different context than child entertainers.

Further, it is doubtful that those who lobbied for an exception to child-labor laws for child actors intended to exempt children in reality programming. This is because defenders of the exemption focused on stage acting. It was urged that the theater, "with its lessons of history, costume, and custom . . . is a liberal education . . . [thus] in going to the stage [the child] is going to school [taken from Viviana A. Zelizer's *Pricing the Priceless Child*]." The rationale behind this—that children's work should be limited to enriching activities that nourish the mind, body, soul, and character—guided the determination of which occupations would remain free from child-labor-law prohibition.

This rationale, of course, does not apply to children forced to live their actual lives in a televised fishbowl with their real-life heartaches offered as fodder for others' amusement. It is thus doubtful that those who advocated for the exception for child actors intended to include children in reality programming.

Original intent notwithstanding, the plain language of the definition of a "performer" includes children in reality programming. It is, therefore, very likely that the FLSA does not protect these children from the harms caused by participating in reality programming since these children are swept within the FLSA's exemption for actors and performers.

State Laws Are Insufficient

Numerous states also have child labor laws. Unlike the FLSA, many even protect child performers. These laws are insufficient, however, to remedy the unique problems posed by reality programming.

What a Court Ruling on Child Labor on Reality Programming Might Entail

A finding that child participation on a reality program is regulable under the FLSA [Fair Labor Standards Act] will have a major impact on who producers and networks can hire, how [a reality] show is produced, and when the children can participate. First, all children fourteen years old and younger would be prohibited from participating. Second, in order for fourteen- and fifteen-year-olds to participate, the Secretary of Labor would have to find that such participation does not interfere with their well-being or the employers would have to comply with the various limitations placed on employing fourteen- and fifteen-year-olds. And in the event that the Secretary permits the participation, the children would only be allowed to work specified and limited hours. Third, all minors would be prohibited from activities deemed "particularly hazardous." Finally, FLSA coverage would guarantee that reality children receive the Act's minimum wage and overtime protections. FLSA coverage would not supplant state child labor laws that are more protective than the federal regulations. FLSA coverage would, however, force employers who may want to film in states with lax child labor laws to comply with the federal standards.

Adam P. Greenberg, "Reality's Kids: Are Children
Who Participate on Reality Television Shows
Covered under the Fair Labor Standards Act?,"
Southern California Law Review, 2009.

First, state labor laws do not clearly apply to children in reality programming. Three states with important connections to the entertainment industry, California, New York, and Florida, have laws that may apply to children in reality programming, as do other states, but the extent of their protection is uncertain.

Even if some states enacted such laws, it would not suffice because producers can evade individual state laws by filming in other states. Unlike traditional entertainment, reality programming typically does not require elaborate sets and studios and may occur anywhere. Parents seeking to profit from their children may even move to different states for more favorable laws.

Even if all states enacted identical statutes, forum shopping would not end. State statutes are subject to interpretation and enforcement by the judicial and executive branches of the individual states. This fact alone will inevitably create variation among state laws. Specific state laws are therefore insufficient, and a federal statute is necessary to provide uniformity and consistency. . . .

A Congressional Statute Is Needed

Congress should provide that, notwithstanding the FLSA or other law, children under a specified age may not appear in reality programming. The statute could define "reality programming" as it is defined in this article, as a format of entertainment in which individuals are employed to be filmed for profit (whether funds are paid to them, their parents, or others on their behalf) as they engage in purportedly unscripted activities. It would not include isolated instances where children appear for less than one hour of total appearance time on camera in a program. This caveat ensures that children who are merely ancillary figures needed to tell stories are not prohibited from participating in a limited fashion. Such limited participation should not bring the harmful consequences . . . that repeat exposure, which destroys privacy, causes. Reality programming would encompass whatever media is used to disseminate such programming, such as television (cable and broadcast), movies, DVDs, and the Internet.

Congress could investigate and hold hearings to determine the appropriate age for prohibition. It might consult with child psychologists and others to determine at what point in development appearing in reality programming becomes least harmful. With this in mind, Congress should develop a sliding scale of prohibition and regulation. For example, from infancy to age

15, no participation; ages 16 and 17, participation is permissible subject to regulation regarding conditions of employment; age 18 and over, no regulation. This option is ideal because it enables Congress to enact a clear statute with an express pronouncement regarding employing children in reality programming.

Organizations to Contact

The editors have compiled the following list of organizations concerned with the issues debated in this book. The descriptions are derived from materials provided by the organizations. All have publications or information available for interested readers. The list was compiled on the date of publication of the present volume; the information provided here may change. Be aware that many organizations take several weeks or longer to respond to inquiries, so allow as much time as possible.

American Civil Liberties Union (ACLU)
125 Broad Street, 18th Floor
New York, NY 10004
(212) 549-2500
website: www.aclu.org

In its work as an organization dedicated to ensuring that the rights of all individuals around the world are observed, the ACLU has paid special attention to the rights of children and young people, a group whose rights have historically been ignored. In particular, labor laws have been one focus of the organization. The ACLU website provides links to significant human rights treaties guaranteeing the rights of children and current action being taken by the organization relating to child labor rights.

American Federation of Labor and Congress of Industrial Organizations (AFL-CIO)
815 16th Street, NW
Washington, DC 20006
website: www.aflcio.org

The AFL-CIO is a federation of various workers unions from around the country, including teachers, firefighters, engineers, doctors, and more. The organization works to ensure that the individuals in all of these fields have ample opportunities to improve their lives and have a voice in the national debate concerning workers' rights. With regards to child labor, the AFL-CIO continues to serve as a watchdog for minors' employee rights and educate the public about child labor's history and consequences. Current information and commentary on state and federal legislation regarding child labor rights are available on the organization's website.

American Youth Policy Forum (AYPF)
1836 Jefferson Place, NW
Washington, DC 20036
(202) 775-9731 • fax: (202) 775-9733
e-mail: aypf@aypf.org
website: www.aypf.org

AYPF has been working since its founding in 1993 to aid young people in fulfilling their potential in academics, employment, and civic life by encouraging policy makers to implement policies that advance these goals. To ensure the achievement of this mission, AYPF focuses its efforts on young adult employment training to educate both youth and government officials about the current issues in youth employment and the steps that need to be taken to ensure that young Americans have the opportunity to work and contribute to society. Numerous reports and issue briefs on youth employment issues can be read on the AYPF website.

Anti-Slavery International
Thomas Clarkson House
The Stableyard, Broomgrove Road
London, SW9 9TL, UK
44 (0)20 7501 8920 • fax: 44 (0)20 7738 4110
e-mail: info@antislavery.org

website: www.antislavery.org

Anti-Slavery International is a charity based in the United Kingdom that works on local, national, and international levels to eradicate slavery worldwide. Reports about child labor in individual countries, slavery, and trafficking, among other topics, can be read on the organization's website.

The Child Labor Coalition (CLC)

1701 K Street, NW, Suite 1200
Washington, DC 20006
website: www.stopchildlabor.org

The National Consumers League founded the CLC in 1989 as an organization devoted to the elimination of abuses of child labor worldwide and the protection of teen workers' rights and welfare. The website provides information about child labor practices around the world and updates about consumer products in the United States produced either directly by child labor or with materials originating from child laborers. Additionally, information about current child labor guidelines in the United States can be found in articles such as "DOL on Its Proposed Child-Safety Rules for US Agriculture."

Child Labor Public Education Project

Labor Center, University of Iowa
100 Bio Ventures Center, Room W130
Iowa City, IA 52242
(319) 335-4144 • fax: (319) 335-4464
e-mail: labor-center@uiowa.edu
website: www.continuetolearn.uiowa.edu/laborctr
/child_labor

The Child Labor Public Education Project at the University of Iowa seeks to provide information about the harmful effects of child labor on children and societies around the globe.

Information about the United States' history of child labor, international agreements, and societal impacts of child labor is available on the project's website.

Human Rights Watch (HRW)

350 Fifth Ave., 34th Floor
New York, NY 10118-3299
(212) 290-4700
website: www.hrw.org

As an international organization that aims to preserve human rights worldwide, HRW has focused special attention on ensuring that the rights of employed minors are protected. Through its educational and advocacy-based programs, HRW seeks to shed light on abuse of child labor and provide concerted action to halt it. Articles on the organization's website such as "Child Farmworkers in the United States: A 'Worst Form of Child Labor'" and "Child Labor and Our Groceries" highlight current child labor rights abuses.

Institute for Agriculture and Trade Policy (IATP)

2105 First Ave. South
Minneapolis, MN 55404
(612) 870-0453 • fax: (612) 870-4846
website: www.iatp.org

Based in the United States, IATP works on both local and global levels to promote fair and sustainable agricultural systems and trade. One facet of this mission is to inform the public about agricultural child labor around the world and the products this labor produces. Articles such as "The Travesty of Child Labor" and "Food Sleuth: Child Labor Chocolate Isn't Sweet" can be read on the IATP website.

International Labor Organization (ILO)

4 Route des Morillons, CH-1211

Genève 22, Switzerland
41 (0)22 799 6111 • fax: 41 (0)22 798 8685
e-mail: ilo@ilo.org
website: www.ilo.org

ILO is the United Nations agency dedicated to the promotion of fair labor standards and policies worldwide. The organization's program on youth employment focuses its efforts on assisting countries to ensure that their labor practices for children are in accordance with human rights standards and on assisting countries that already observe these standards to develop policies that will reverse the current trend of youth unemployment. It also runs the International Programme on the Elimination of Child Labour, which addresses the issue of child labor on an international level. ILO's website provides extensive information about this program and resources on youth employment in general, including reports such as *Global Employment Trends for Youth* and *Policy Options to Support Young Workers During Economic Recovery.*

National Youth Rights Association (NYRA)
1101 15th Street NW, Suite 200
Washington, DC 20005
(202) 835-1739
website: www.youthrights.org

NYRA is a youth-led national non-profit organization dedicated to fighting for the civil rights and liberties of young people. NYRA has members in all fifty states—more than seven thousand members in total. It seeks to lower the voting age, lower the drinking age, repeal curfew laws, and protect student rights.

US Department of Labor (DOL)
200 Constitution Avenue, NW
Washington, DC 20210
(866) 487-2365
website: www.dol.gov

DOL is the US government agency charged with ensuring that workers in the United States receive fair compensation and that their employers provide them with necessary benefits and working conditions. As such, one area of focus is the rights and safety of youth workers. Reports detailing current statistics on youth workers in the United States can be found on DOL's website, along with links to information about agricultural youth employment, international child labor, state laws and other topics.

US Equal Employment Opportunity Commission (EEOC)

131 M Street, NE
Washington, DC 20507
(202) 663-4900
website: www.eeoc.gov

The EEOC is a US federal government agency created to ensure that employees in the United States are not subjected to discrimination in the workplace. Youth @ Work is the commission's website dedicated to providing information about young workers' rights and responsibilities. Details of recent cases regarding teen claims of discrimination can be viewed on the site as well as fact sheets about young workers' rights.

Workplace Fairness (WF)

920 U Street, NW
Washington, DC 20001
(202) 683-6114 • fax: (240) 282-8801
website: www.workplacefairness.org

WF works to ensure that workers' rights are protected and observed in workplaces across the country by educating individuals and those who advocate on their behalf about these rights. WF covers topics such as hiring, discrimination, and pay, among others. The WF website provides articles such as "Summertime, and the Working Isn't Easy" focusing specifically on the rights of teen workers.

Young Workers United

215 Golden Gate Avenue, PO Box 420963
San Francisco, CA 94142
(415) 621-4155
e-mail: youngworkersunited@gmail.com
website: www.youngworkersunited.org

Young Workers United is a membership organization based in San Francisco that seeks to improve the working conditions and wages of employees in the low-wage service sector and ensure that workers' rights are always observed. They provide educational information about workers' rights and seek to expose those businesses and individuals that fail to maintain an employment environment in accordance with these rights.

For Further Reading

Books

Randall K.Q. Ackee, Eric V. Edmonds, and Konstantinos Tatsiramos, *Child Labor and the Transition Between School and Work*. Bingley, UK: Emerald, 2010.

David G. Blanchflower and Richard B. Freeman, *Youth Employment and Joblessness in Advanced Countries*. Chicago: University of Chicago Press, 2000.

Holly Cullen, *The Role of International Law in the Elimination of Child Labor*. Boston: Martinus Nijhoff, 2007.

Valentina Forastieri, *Children at Work: Health and Safety Risks*. Geneva: ILO, 2002.

Raymond G. Fuller, *Child Labor and the Constitution*. New York: Arno, 1974.

Christiaan Grootaert and Harry Anthony Patrinos, *The Policy Analysis of Child Labor: A Comparative Study*. New York: St. Martin's, 1999.

Windy Herumin, *Child Labor Today: A Human Rights Issue*. Berkeley Heights, NJ: Enslow, 2008.

Hugh D. Hindman, ed., *Child Labor: An American History*. Armonk, NY: M.E. Sharpe, 2002.

———, *The World of Child Labor: An Historical and Regional Survey*. Armonk, NY: M.E. Sharpe, 2009.

Marvin J. Levine, *Children for Hire: the Perils of Child Labor in the United States*. Westport, CT: Praeger, 2003.

Clark Nardinelli, *Child Labor and the Industrial Revolution*. Bloomington: Indiana University Press, 1990.

Ian C. Rivera and Natasha M. Howard, eds., *Child Labor in America*. New York: Nova Science, 2010.

Shelley Sallee, *The Whiteness of Child Labor Reform in the New South*. Athens: University of Georgia Press, 2004.

James D. Schmidt, *Industrial Violence and the Legal Origins of Child Labor*. New York: Cambridge University Press, 2010.

Ronald B. Taylor, *Sweatshops in the Sun: Child Labor on the Farm*. Boston: Beaon, 1973.

William G. Whittaker, *The Fair Labor Standards Act*. New York: Novinka Books, 2003.

Periodicals and Internet

David Bacon, "Mexico's New Braceros," *Nation*, January 27, 1997.

Marylin Bender Altschul, "Exploiting the Model Child," *The Nation*, September 15, 1962.

David Bennett, "Agriculture Facing Major Changes in Child Labor Laws," *Southwest Farm Press*, September 15, 2011.

Ana Campoy and Schott Kilman, "Farmers Contest Child-Labor Rules," *Wall Street Journal*, December 5, 2011.

Scott J. Cech, "Child-Labor Proposal Eyes Private Model," *Education Week*, June 6, 2007.

Peter Edelman, "Child Labor Revisited," *The Nation*, August 21, 1982.

Marion Herbert, "Getting Students off Farms and into Classrooms," *District Administration*, July 2011.

Human Rights Watch, "United States: Adopt Stronger Laws for Child Farmworkers," September 14, 2009. www.hrw.org.

Katherine Johnson, "Confronting Child Labor," *Primary and Middle Years Educator*, October 2005.

Jesse Kline, "Kids at Work," *Reason*, October 2010.

Douglas Kruse and Douglas Mahony, "Illegal Child Labor in the United States: Prevalence and Characteristics," National Bureau of Economic Research Working Paper #6479, March 1998. www.nber.org.

Lindsay Lieberman, "Protecting Pageant Princesses: A Call for Statutory Regulation of Child Beauty Pageants," *Journal of Law and Policy*, 2010.

Terry E. Lockett, "Remembering Lewis Hine," *The Humanist*, September–October 2011.

Kari Lydersen, "Missouri Legislator Wants to Increase Child Labor," *In These Times*, February 25, 2011. www.inthese times.com.

Ian Millhiser, "Sen. Mike Lee Calls Child Labor Laws Unconstitutional," *Think Progress*, January 14, 2011. www .thinkprogress.org.

Carolyn M. Moehling, "State Child Labor Laws and the Decline of Child Labor," *Explorations in Economic History*, January 1999.

Sy Moskowitz, "American Youth in the Workplace: Legal Aberration, Failed Social Policy," *Albany Law Review*, 2004.

Shawn Zeller, "Getting Out of Chores," *CQ Weekly*, November 7, 2011.

Index